SAMUEL GOMPERS—
AMERICAN STATESMAN

SAMUEL GOMPERS

27 January, 1850—13 December, 1924

SAMUEL GOMPERS—
AMERICAN STATESMAN

FLORENCE CALVERT THORNE

DISCARDED

GREENWOOD PRESS, PUBLISHERS
NEW YORK

Contents

Foreword

I first met Samuel Gompers in the summer of 1910. That meeting was one of a series of academic accidents. My two years at Oberlin College had been filled with requirements for an A.B. degree, including Latin and Greek, and modernized a bit by Anglo-Saxon, Middle English and then Chaucer, chosen mainly because the courses were given by an authority in that field. Greek, Latin and Early English courses brought a taste and a background for history, in which I later specialized at the University of Chicago, supplemented by courses in political science given by Charles Edward Merriam who taught government as a living institution. A brief course in economic theory decided me that it would not help me much in getting at the facts of life. As I was registering for my last quarter of undergraduate work Dean Breckenridge mentioned a course in trade unionism given by Robert F. Hoxie, whom she recommended as one of the best teachers in the University. Here I found history in the making as Professor Hoxie taught it. I supplemented that course by signing for Dr. Hoxie's seminar in trade unions and elected for my assignment a term paper on the American Federation of Labor in Politics. The most valuable data were in the minds and experiences of those who had lived trade unionism.

One Saturday morning I was up early and on the Illinois Central, reviewing a series of questions which I planned to put to George W. Perkins, President of the Cigarmakers International Union, to get more clues to information needed for my thesis. But Mr. Perkins had to do his editorials for his cigarmakers' monthly journal and met my obvious disappointment with the news: "Sam is in town. You need to talk to him anyhow." "Where?" said I with the zeal of the inexperienced. I called the hotel. A voice with the volume of a pipe organ answered. "Have breakfast with me here at eleven o'clock." Such hours are convenient! thought I, for my seven-thirty breakfast in Green Hall had long ended its service. Over to the old Briggs Hotel I hastened. Arriving in advance of the time appointed I watched Chicago labor men as they moved about the lobby. Some I recognized, as attendance and reporting on the meetings of the Chicago Federation of Labor were required of students taking Dr. Hoxie's course in trade unions. Finally the door of the elevator opened on a short, squat figure in a buttoned Prince Albert coat. His short legs moved with extreme dignity, and with a courtly gesture he invited me into the dining room.

The unhurried interview lasted about three hours and ended with this offer: Come to Washington and all the files of the Federation will be available to you. When I reported to Dr. Hoxie, his comment was: How soon can you go? This is an unparalleled offer.

Gompers was a fascinating personality. His powerful eyes and resonant voice which served his many purposes so well directed attention away from his physical incongruities as he told me of his life, his difficulties and his plans. Although obviously a man of great personal pride and ambition, he had dedicated himself and all his abilities to service for his fellow workers. He wanted them to have what he valued most—individual liberty. He told how wage-earners were being denied constitutional rights by the courts and by Congress. The whole experience was to me profoundly appealing, as I had been reared in the traditions of a family that came to the new world to found a colony where all might have freedom to worship in accord with their consciences. A later generation furnished pioneers for the Middle West. My father, the son of a Georgia planter, had given four years to what meant to him the cause of local self-government. As the South had lost most of its capital many of its young men followed the pioneers north, west or southwest.

Labor's cause, as Mr. Gompers told it, appealed to

me as pioneering in a new field. As soon as possible I went to Washington to complete my thesis, and so began a new discipline in my own education. My first summer spent in the offices of the American Federation of Labor convinced me one could not understand trade unions by reading about them in libraries but one must observe them in action, learn what they did, how they did it and why. At the time of my arrival the Executive Council was in session. I was intrigued by the atmosphere of concentrated deference and respect which hovered over the office and focussed all activity on its presence and needs. Perhaps the personality of Mr. Gompers' secretary encouraged appreciation of significances of the constructive and spiritual meaning of trade unions. She was a frail little person of a good Virginia family whose life was dedicated to service of her Chief. She permitted herself to see only his virtues and great service to mankind.

Mr. Gompers seemed anxious I should have sources. Each individual file had to have the Chief's personal inspection and explanation. Research in the Federation files was as new to the Federation staff as to me. Mr. Gompers made good on his promise to open everything. He formed a habit of dropping in as he passed by my door to see what I was doing and to make suggestions. As he fingered lovingly the old records, he told me stories about each, reliving episodes in Federation history. He told me not only what he did but often why he did it so I could follow his mind through problems that recurred in the successive years. He occasionally referred with obvious pride to the instruction in trade unionism which he gave me. It was an invaluable seminar. The clearcut body of principles that guided his decisions is important in understanding the policies of this man who was the vital center of the American Federation of Labor in its founding years.

Intellectually he was honest and undeviating. As a man of action and a participant in our complex society, he had many personalities many of which I did not know or caught only glimpses. His constituency were the lowly, the makers and users of tools, the more recent immigrants in the process of induction into American citizenship—the

most numerous single national group. The future of the
nation was conditioned by whether they adopted American
ways of life or whether they shifted directions. That
America was his vision and ideal, that he modelled the
constitution and procedures of the American labor movement after those of the U.S.A., that he made freedom
the compass guiding the progress of this numerically major
national group, that he taught them to revere and help
strengthen institutions rooted in personal freedom and
private property and to honor responsibilities accompany-
ing personal rights, entitles him to rank among the founders
of our nation.

His work as a constructive, conservative leader of
millions of Americans is his enduring contribution to this
country and the world period in which he lived, which
places him high among American statesmen.

The public and private philosophy which directed
this leadership and the principles on which its growth
was squared are important in understanding the past and
planning the future. This information is in files, archives
and libraries, but not readily available for all those who
may want it.

For many years I had the privilege of working with
him in confidential capacity, first as an editorial and
research assistant and as writing assistant when he prepared
his autobiography. He used to say to me: "Girl, if you
want to work with me you must understand what is in
my mind."

As I had an unusual opportunity to study Gompers'
mind and to learn why he did what he did I feel an
obligation to him to record what he taught me and to
make available the results of my observation and study
during the over twelve years I worked with him as a
confidential assistant and later noted how his policies
endured under succeeding leadership and changing conditions. This compilation does not make the slightest claim
to be anything but the report of a person who observed
forces that shaped the history of this national institution
at close range for a number of years. It is in no sense

official or interpretative for purposes of evaluation but tries to picture a powerful personality in action as he would wish to be recorded.

His fixed practice was to have present at every conference he had on Federation matters either an official of the Federation or a confidential assistant. His purpose was always to have a source for confirmation or for recording—verbal or otherwise. He asked me to sit in on many fascinating important conferences with individuals and groups.

During the years in which he was active he spoke often and wrote much so that reiteration of principles and points of view indicates the relative importance of principles in his basic philosophy. Selected quotations bring the reader in direct contact with Mr. Gompers' mind and personality with the minimum intervention of interpretation by the author. Care has been exercised to select the typical and significant.

I express grateful appreciation to John Philip Frey for reading and making suggestions on manuscript, to Margaret Scattergood for help in finding and selecting quotations and to Ralph Ainsley Anderson for critical editorial reading. Mr. Frey is the only living member of the group of pioneer trade unionists whose counsel Mr. Gompers sought and trusted over several decades. His suggestions on facts and significant developments have been most important.

The librarian of the U.S. Department of Labor, Margaret F. Brickett, and her staff have been most generous in making their materials available.

Florence Calvert Thorne

McLean, Virginia

SAMUEL GOMPERS—
AMERICAN STATESMAN

1. Who Was Samuel Gompers?

Who was Samuel Gompers?

Born in East Side London, he lived his first thirteen years in a one room apartment with city streets for boys' sports and activities. His primary schooling in the neighborhood Jewish school ended at the age of ten. His parents were born in Holland—his father of the Dutch branch of the Gomperz family which was scattered through many European countries and his mother Sarah Root. They brought to London Dutch cooking customs and possessions. At ten the boy had to add his mite to family income. He first tried shoemaking. Annoyed by the noise, he asked his father to teach him cigarmaking. But still there was not enough for the family and talk of going to America began. Their French neighbor silk-weavers were overwhelmed by unemployment due to new machines. Their hopeless despair sank deep into the boy's spirit, as he listened to their lament "God strike me dead. My children are hungry and I have no work." Against this background of woe all of East Side London was seething with discussion of the "war to end slavery" as they understood it, and the singing of the popular songs of the time, "The Slave Ship," "To the West, To the Land of the Free." The sympathy of London wage-earners was with the Union and against official aid to the Confederacy and trade with the South. The British Cigarmakers Society had a fund used to help cigarmakers to emigrate. After much talk and discussion the Gompers family decided to go to America.

The family secured passage in a sailing vessel, set out from London June 10, 1863 and were on the water seven weeks and a day. Shipping quarters were cramped and all cooking was done in the ship's galley. They arrived at Castle Garden to find New York disturbed by riots

1

over conscriptions and Negro lynchings. Through friends they found a four-room apartment on Houston street— a material betterment over the one-room London home though the environment and the community life were very similar. Young Gompers began learning the street life of East Side New York and the ways and opportunities of America which to him was ever an ideal. He found and joined boys' clubs, debating societies, fraternal organizations, law study, Cooper Union—a few of the agencies that taught him American ways and ideals. He was young, strong, eager to learn anything and everything, fond of music and people.

The union had always been a factor in family life and young Gompers belonged as a habit, without concern for what the union was or expectation of any benefit from dues payments.

Gompers married early and was at first absorbed in family responsibilities. He tried to resist taking an active part in union affairs or involvement in union affairs or in union policies and administration in order to have time for study, music and for his family. He even tried living outside New York City. That failed and he returned to live in the midst of a motley community of European immigrants, including refugees who had fled failures in revolutions in Europe, or were fugitives because of activity in international organizations and wanted to "liberalize" and Europeanize the new world. So while he learned America, he was kept aware of thought and undertakings current in older countries from which came our culture and our institutions. From then on the trade union became the great fact of his life.

The New York cigarmakers were mainly from the following nationalities—German, Hungarian, English and American, who were connected with English, German and Bohemian speaking sections of the United Cigarmakers and coordinated by an over-all council. Each national division fixed its own requirements for union membership. Having seen so many trade unions fail in time of need or lose their members between strikes, self-appointed cigarmakers determined to devise an organization that would provide continuing services for its members as well as assist the workers during special efforts to better terms and conditions of work.

There were two main systems of work: the tenement and the turn-in. Under the first, the employer owned the tenements and rented apartments to cigarmakers who turned their living space into workshops where they and their whole family worked. Each man bought his tobacco supplies from his employer, furnished his own tools and was paid for cigars made, sometimes in scrip redeemable in the employer's store. The "turn-in" system also permitted the cigarmakers to work at home. They bought supplies from the industrials with whom they deposited about twice the value of the supplies. The cigarmakers expected to return cigars to the proprietor of the warehouse who not infrequently closed his warehouse for weeks, or found excessive fault with the cigars or refused to take them at all. Then the cigarmakers had to sell directly to retailers. Stringent internal revenue regulation ended the turn-in-job system and encouraged factory production, a method that suggested to the union how to remedy the tenement evil. As Samuel Gompers grew older he found a job in a factory—a union factory.

The active union cigarmakers determined to deal with these problems. They proceeded by study of existing practices to discussion of proposals for betterment. All agreed the union was the agency that promised hope, and concurred with equal unanimity they must create a new kind of union suited to workers' needs in this country. Most of the existing unions organized by immigrants followed the practices of their old, home country—that was service only as a fraternal and discussion group. So S.G., Adolph Strasser, Karl Laurrell and other cigarmakers set about this task with vigor and idealism. One of their first undertakings was to end or regulate tenement production by state law, as a health measure. Samuel Gompers was selected to get information to make the case for such regulation. Disguised as a book agent, he talked with many families and recorded facts on production conditions in tenements. That done, the union leaders began to discuss specific plans.

They realized that representative institutions and civil rights constituted a basic difference between European countries and the United States. Initiative and individual responsibility were qualities required to transform nature's wilderness into homes of persons accustomed to civilized life and all had shared the common struggle with the wilderness to secure supplies for existence. Ability to meet common hazards constituted a rough standard for evaluating individuals and one which served to discourage artificial barriers. Community customs were rooted in these individual qualities.

The story of how an American local union of cigarmakers was created is recorded in Seventy Years of Life and Labor. The union had been reorganized with each new strike and then allowed to decline into inexpensive ghosthood until another strike was unavoidable. There was no considered development of union demands, with formal presentation and discussion with employers in advance of action. When grievance became too sore, someone arose and announced: "I am going on strike. Who will join me?" Usually all workers rose and walked out after the strike leader. The only union discipline consisted in response to all such strike calls and in resentment against scabs. Strike leaders usually failed to get their jobs back. The group's first conclusion was that the union could be much more than an adjunct of strikes when sustained by regularly paid dues and by members who believed the union was a way of life. If union executives were authorized to conduct the union like a business undertaking, and to study industry and economic developments so as to time union policies they could utilize union funds so as to provide the members with services and welfare aids during emergencies. Union funds properly administered would provide more and more adequate services.

As hand tools provided quiet for discussion during work, the cigarmakers talked over problems and plans while they worked or paid one of the members to read to them. They increased their understanding of their problems, they decided to abandon what S. G. called a Cheap-John unionism.

Reading and discussion led to better informed judgments on demands for wage increases and shorter hours. Agents for collective bargaining (union executives) were selected with greater care. With more information of the state of the industry it became obvious how collective bargaining could be developed and conducted more effectively. Workers and employers began to learn the economy of avoiding strikes.

It is important to realize the significance of establishing the union contract as the primary agency for wage-earner progress. It is the tap root from which economic unionism as a constituent element in a market economy grew. Here began the basic union leadership that safeguarded the most numerous group of America's citizens against socialist-communist collectivist theories and ideals.

The development of a stable union led to the establishment of the practice of conferences of union representatives of the workers with their employers to agree upon hours and pay standards. As contracts are the agency which control practically all other business relationships, union contracts accustomed workers to normal business relations and enabled them to participate in free markets on the same basis as other participating elements. The union became their business agent in addition to its responsibility of providing for political, educational and creative needs of the workers. The cigarmakers became acquainted with the major problems of all wage-earners and worked out some methods of dealing with them.

The early cigarmakers union admitted only skilled workers who learned their trade by serving an apprenticeship under the supervision of craftsmen with whom they worked. Strippers, bunch breakers, mold users and other unskilled workers, usually women workers, were at first not considered eligible, and got recognition and admission only as technical changes and tools greatly increased the proportion of those excluded.

First these union builders evolved a draft constitution for the local union which prescribed eligibility for members, the machinery of union government, union functions, union dues, election machinery, etc. The committee provided each union member with a copy of this basic union law. This was a precedent in union operation —now a matter of course. The committee with the help of a jelly-pad for duplication and their own willing hands provided this first tool for self-government which then proceeded through education and experimentation. A condition which facilitated the endeavor and which its leaders benefitted by to the utmost was the absence of noise in the workshop—no pounding, no whir of wheels, no sudden work crisis in which voices needed to be raised. There was unrestricted opportunity for discussion, presentation of ideas, reading and other ways of keeping minds active. Out of it came a progressive strong local union with such services as an employment bureau, fraternal benefits, strike benefits, aids for collective bargaining. There was active interest and participation in work of the union and a healthy feeling of loyalty for its interests and welfare.

Then this same group turned its attention to expanding this constructive development throughout the industry. They elected A. Strasser president of the National Cigarmakers Union, Samuel Gompers vice president, and revised its constitution. Next they set about making the constitution into a living, functioning organization to promote the welfare of all cigarmakers throughout the industry.

All officers were elective and all members had equal right to vote. National officers were at first elected by conventions but later, in what was then considered a step to greater democracy, this decision also was referred to individual membership vote. The right to vote was considered evidence of democracy and a paid-up union card vouched for the worker's eligibility as a craftsman as well as his fraternal affiliation.

The union card became a sort of passport that introduced a member wherever he travelled or sought work away from home base. Later it became the authentic "countersign" as it were between unions and served as official verbal communication between unions. Such talismanic uses gave the union card symbolic significance.

All commonplace procedures, record keeping and habits of doing union business had to be developed and standardized as unions grew and did more and more. All of these functions and procedures were unified and built into organizational structures. They seemed simple and matter of course later, but first they had to be thought through, selected and then made part of union organization.

As they made the Cigarmakers National Union one of the foremost craft organizations of the country, they were constantly aware of the subtle competition between standards of various other industries and the need for understanding between all national unions of craftsmen and wage-earning associations. The movement for national organization of other craft unions was well under way.

Next cigarmakers found that they had problems which also concerned workers in other industries and that a federation of national trade unions could do for workers a service analogous to what our federal government does for citizens of various states. At least one national over-all organization of wage-earners and a number of political organizations of Labor had existed previously but none proved effective or permanent. The cigarmakers group took a leading responsibility in calling and organizing the Federation of Trades and Labor Unions of the United States and Canada in 1881.

The first Federation (1881-6) was modelled after the British Trades Union Congress, without full-time officers and with emphasis on legislation. When the Knights of Labor attempted to absorb trade unions and invaded their right of self-government the cigarmakers were leaders in the rebellion which brought reorganization of the Federation and started the decline of the Knights of Labor. Samuel Gompers was elected its full-time president with instructions to give all his time, with a promise of a salary of $1,000 but no funds to pay anything—not even rent or office expenses. With the exception of one year he was annually re-elected president until his death in 1924. The continuity of his responsibility gives added importance to Gompers' thinking and the principles that guided his leadership.

The Executives of the American Federation of Labor consisted of a President, a Secretary and a Treasurer. These officers, together with an Executive Council, functioned variously: as a Court of Appeals, a Supreme Court, as consultative, planning authority, etc.

The final authority of the Federation was lodged in annual conventions in which national trade unions were represented in proportion to membership and all American Federation of Labor regional organizations in accord with fixed provisions which safeguarded the autonomy of national trade unions. The convention reviewed the work of the year, decided upon new undertakings, elected all officers and representatives and provided for the succeeding convention. National and international unions had full and final authority within their jurisdictions—that is, upon economic matters including qualifications for membership, collective bargaining, strikes, benefits, etc.

The Federation's responsibilities were over-all labor problems and policies, relationships between unions, activities that required unified planning and action, relationships to public policy and agencies, representation in world-wide labor matters, etc. Within the economic field the Federation was to serve as the coordinator of policy and action, and to make provision for representation in various projects affecting two or more national trade unions. Checks upon arbitrary decisions were afforded by various provisions for appeal as well as for re-opening of issues for consideration and action by recurring conventions.

A roll-call vote on some issues such as amendments to the constitution was required—in which national and international unions cast votes proportional to membership. Roll-call on other matters could be had by vote of one-tenth of the delegates present. Central bodies and directly affiliated unions had one vote each.

The American Federation of Labor carefully provided for continuity with the organization it superseded and assumed its debts and other responsibilities. Continuity with the past history and traditions is necessary to individuals and living organizations.

Samuel Gompers in preparing for the reorganization

of the Federation, studied and debated with his associates the official record of the debates within the U.S. Constitutional Convention as kept by James Madison and the unofficial notes made public later. As in the formulation of the United States Constitution the basic problem was how to get a national organization strong enough to provide unity necessary for a responsible government while at the same time preserving for functional subdivisions freedom for action within their jurisdiction or trade autonomy. The United States Constitution provides separation of powers into executive, legislative and judicial co-equal divisions, to assure balance within government and checks on usurpation of unauthorized power. The Federation Constitution provided for adjustment of inter-union conflicts and protected trade autonomy with appeal to the Federation hierarchy—president, executive council and convention—and prescribed functions for regional organizations. There were two main differences: The Federation had no means of coercion except disassociation which was in itself self-defeating, and national craft organizations could carry their economic functions beyond geographic political borders and develop local units (unions) in other countries. The Federation found its responsibility for maintenance of law and order between national and international trade unions a major and ever-developing preoccupation.

The conditions which necessitated reorganization of the Federation led to special emphasis on an organization of workers, by workers, to deal with economic problems and interests. This organization became the strongest economic organization of workers in the world.

The Knights of Labor with a large membership of workers, employers and good-intentioned wishers for co-operation between individuals of all manner of interests, fell into the hands of individuals who wanted power and saw that the Knights could quickly gain political power by taking over economic functions of trade unions dealing with employers, calling strikes, etc. As door bell ringers and couriers against such aggression and invasion of trade union rights, cigarmakers and others hurried from union to union and wrote communications to more distant ones until union officials were made fully aware of the need for protective action.

Out of pressing need to resist efforts to dominate labor on two fronts—efforts of the Knights of Labor to use trade unions for their organizational purposes and program on the one hand, and persistent efforts of the Socialist Party members to infiltrate unions to increase advocates of the Socialist program and induce workers to vote the Socialist Party into control of the Government, S. G. developed through the Federation a program of "pure and simple" trade unionism—a distinctively American institution. The basic unit of the Federation was the trade union whose union card was a certification of craft skill of members and automatically restricted membership to workers with the same problems, the same purposes and the same needs.

American wage earners worked in an economy busy with the development and exploration of its economic resources and later expanding rapidly with the evolution of modern large scale industries as techniques of mass production followed the application of mechanical power—first steam, then electric—that replaced hand tools until agriculture was no longer our dominant way of life. Free trade unions united for economic purposes, were flexible enough to adapt to the revolutionary changes in their work and to make progress with the other elements in production. The industrial development started a trend toward concentration of population in urban centers with relative decline on farms, thus increasing the dependence of all on the prosperity of urban industries.

There was much in the spirit and the physical conditions of our country that strengthened individualism in all groups. There was the common need to take possession of the continent and to organize its resources for the Nation's use. Dangers, hardships and need for creative ingenuity developed qualities making for national vigor and progress. There was no question of government taking over and regimenting. Need stimulated resourcefulness to contrive all manner of voluntary associations, and to adjust and adapt these instrumentalities until they produced satisfactory results. Even yet, in many regions we are close to the pioneer spirit that was ready and capable of endurance and of coping with new situations.

Employers as well as workers in the early days were individualists who took great pride in the products of their industry, daring and resourcefulness. They had not always learned to respect the rights of others in order to retain their own and to promote the general welfare in order to buttress permanence in individual achievements. Consequently efforts on the part of workers to establish recognition of their rights and mesh the exercise of these rights with the accepted business practices not infrequently resulted in violence and direct action very akin to civil war. But somehow after the warfare ceased, a feeling of kindredship in a common undertaking developed. The fresh air of the new world put out the smoldering fires that otherwise might have generated class-conscious feelings solidifying into barriers. The spirit of the American trade union movement has had much to do with maintaining this attitude. It was interested in practical measures to raise standards of living and wider opportunities for workers and their families—in sharing benefits not in taking away from others what they had: in increasing their share of increased output, not in taking over controls so as to direct management and distribution.

Mr. Gompers called the trade union the great fact of his life, overshadowing all other interests and bringing them into a new focus and relationship of purposes. He told how Karl Laurrell taught him. "Sam," said he, "hold your trade union card in front of you in deciding all issues and unless they square with it, they aren't good for you." Laurrell's instruction helped to establish in his thinking the trade union as the dependence and ever useful tool of the wage-earner. The union provides for his needs as a worker—apprentice training, employment information and placement, contractual arrangements and enforcement, representation in disputes between workers and management, changes in tools and processes, etc. In addition wage-earners found themselves confronted by new needs and problems as citizens of their locality and community life, or, denied rights and opportunities which should be theirs, they can use their unions to mobilize political power for the correction of specific abuses. With the development of administrative law and huge administrative staffs not responsible to voting citizens, wage-earners whose interests are directly affected need direct representatives to safeguard labor's interests. S.G. helped draft this pattern in the Federal Vocational Education Act giving voluntary organizations previously responsible for a function which government took over, representation in administering the law.

Gompers and the group in which he cooperated recognized that Labor's problems under a representative government were basically different from those of the old world. Workers could share in existing agencies—governmental, political and community—and had equal individual rights and equality before the law. Their task was to avail themselves of existing rights, opportunities and agencies rather than to set up new and rival ones. In other words to share America, rather than attempt to dominate or control or set up rival and divisive institutions.

A powerful individual who loved and respected the ideal which meant America to him served a developing group of citizens during the formative period when they became conscious of their needs, their rights and their obligations. His earliest education was in a Jewish school including some instruction in the Talmud. His earliest thinking was concerned with anti-slavery, unemployment due to new inventions, freedom and opportunity in the new world. He came to the new world familiar with the problems of labor and gave his life to these problems. Mr. Gompers was not an academic student who read widely but those books he read he really studied and they remained with him throughout the years of practical problems. Most of these he met through Cooper Union. While not a learned man, he had rare wisdom distilled from his ability to understand and apply past experience, to gauge the personalities of people, and to utilize individual and collective subconscious.

A startling individual physically — huge torso, short legs, small sensitive hands, magnetic hazel eyes, a pipe-organ voice, responding to his moods and needs for power and emphasis. A born actor, he used all his incongruous parts and gifts to gain and hold attention, and all the other ends necessary to maintain leadership in a voluntary organization and in a society which valued initiative.

America was first his dream world before it became the land of his life work. It was here he strove to make come alive his ideal of wage-earners living as free men with homes providing sanctuary for private living and personal rights, independence and choice in relations with the outside world. That he had the vision to sense the power of spiritual forces in addition to an intuitive wisdom in practical situations and in rousing the will to do among creative leaders, enabled him to build into America's labor movement at the beginning of our industrial age, those basic principles which our pioneer ancestors built into its economic and community institutions and upon which our founding statesmen of the eighteenth century constructed our Republic. These principles shaped and gave meaning to the human structure which was the American Federation of Labor, whose influence became an integral part of our economy with repercussions on employers and unaffiliated workers as well as trade unionists. As wage-earners constitute the "warp and woof" of society, it is fitting that our nation do him the justice and honor of understanding the nature and the quality of the service he gave.

Mr. Gompers modeled the constitution and procedure of the American Federation of Labor after that of the United States because his love and veneration for the United States was such that he wanted the same kind of basic structure to assure effective order in the labor movement. He realized the need for sound basic principles of human relations so as to facilitate united action. The labor movement he believed must be a voluntary organization of wage-earners with mutual problems and common ideals. He put his faith and trust in voluntary principles and never wavered in that course. Over and over again he reminded trade unionists the cure for the evils of democracy is more democracy. He also tried to instil into union practice understanding that rights entailed responsibility for honoring the moral code of western civilization.

In his last years his greatest satisfaction was the love and respect which the rank and file of the labor movement had for him. He had truly dedicated himself to service for his fellow workers and nothing swerved him from union duty and responsibility. He wanted them to have that which he valued most — individual liberty. He wanted wage earners to have opportunity to exercise the constitutional rights assured all American citizens and in addition the right to petition for redress of grievances through the prescribed channels. Gompers saw the labor movement as a basic agency to aid wage-earners to put into use rights available to free human beings. To provide such rights was, he thought, a primary function of government. Use of such basic opportunity was the duty of individuals who accepted their moral responsibility to improve levels of living to give themselves and their dependents better opportunities than they themselves had. He coveted for them life with the dignity of self-determination that can come to those willing to accept responsibility inherent in that way of life. He taught them progress must be earned. By joining hands with like minded workers, they increased proportionately bargaining strength for higher wages which could make more material comforts available out of increased production while personal freedom and self-dependence would help them to be alert and responsible citizens of their community.

These things he said to them publicly and privately, so that contact with him created hope and enthusiasm for the cause.

The American unions developed muscles and direction from their early fights for existence, first against the Knights of Labor, then against the socialist-communist groups — the Socialist Trades and Labor Unions, the American Labor Union, the Industrial Workers of the World, etc. For it should not be forgotten that communist headquarters of the Internationale founded by Karl Marx was transferred to this country and finally dissolved here. As communist and other protest groups initiated revolutionary movements in Europe and failed, some of their leaders sought refuge in this country and continued propaganda here. The force of American ideals in trade unions and the realities of our opportunities repeatedly vanquished this alien philosophy and its leaders. Some of the socialist-communists, assuming protective disguises, infiltrated key offices in unions and created a number of difficult situations, but the strength of the discipline of voluntarism, embedded at the very roots of American trade unionism, has so far protected this Nation against that menace. Communism has found more friendly soil among those without practical experience.

Following the counter revolution in Russia when Lenin and his followers seized control of the government there and set up the soviet system, they simultaneously began planning a world-wide attack on private enterprise and free institutions. A number of communists from Russia were assigned to the United States. Their activities and machinations are still a problem.

The American Federation of Labor proved a dependable and constructive national institution in peace and in war. It demonstrated capacity for practical statesmanship in our economy and in our political practices and traditions. Tested by practical and constructive standards of betterment in work relationships, more comforts in their homes, wider opportunities in community lives of workers, the results were noteworthy.

Samuel Gompers left an enduring monument — a basic economic institution that has grown into the work lives of that numerous group of citizens who are the tool makers and machine users of our technical economy. The institution is a private association adapted to the wage-earner's functions in a market economy and enabling him to function in economic and political government. It was born out of the workers' need for freedom and will serve them as long as they have the will to be free.

From his early years Samuel Gompers accepted the trade union as something inseparable from every wage-earner's life and when he came to know it he made it the great fact of his life. When still young as years were counted but much older in experience, he and a group of fellow-workers dedicated their lives to service through the trade union movement and vowed to accept no public office or preferment that would take them from that service.

As the opportunity for freedom and the practice of freedom were to him inseparable from human dignity and satisfaction in living, he became the leader who likewise believed in freedom and had the courage to make it a way of life. He and the pioneers who worked on his team learned how to develop voluntary associations which wage-earners could operate as channels through which to plan their welfare and share in national life. For over fifty years he was leader in the development of trade unions and for over forty years he was the responsible executive of the national federation of trade unions. Each year he submitted his record of results and his plans for the future to review by a congress of representatives of national trade unions whose endorsement was in the form of election for another year of service. This annual review was a stiff test of leadership not equalled by many leaders of voluntary associations of any groups of citizens.

His was a full life prodigal in its expenditure of himself. Only the most significant policies can be included in a summary. They were his tools for work as his responsibility for leadership developed in the local trade union and extended to the national trade union level, next to federation of unions in the United States and Canada, then to our hemisphere and finally worldwide scope. His work was always some phase of the never-ending need to maintain opportunity for freedom for individuals to exercise their God-given rights for self-development.

As leadership of the American Federation of Labor passed from Samuel Gompers' dead hand and heart, human freedom was its goal and voluntarism its trusted procedure. His last message to American unions was to keep the faith.

2. Why Trade Unions?

For more than four decades Gompers and Trade Unions were synonymous terms to the modern world. Gompers, by appearances, mental traits and by emotional qualities that were springs to action, had a deeper Eastern world heritage than Western though he glorified in Western ideals and institutions. These qualities enabled him to be aware of more phases of human life and to know, to reach and appeal to hidden impulses in a way that engendered most loving personal relationships. He was an ideal leader for the period in which he lived and worked and early found his mission. As he often said, "The trade union was the great fact of my life." He experimented and helped create an American trade union for his craft and then applied the fundamental principles of human relationships to broader fields of work relationship.

In 1889, he gave this explanation of what he was trying to do:

Of all of the struggles of the human family for freedom, order and progress, the trade unions are the direct and legitimate heirs and successors. It is their mission to continue the battle for the right until the term "right" shall lose its relative significance by the abolition of injustice and wrong—to protect the young and innocent, to raise men and women from the sloughs of poverty and despair to a proper appreciation of their rights and duties is worthy of our best efforts, our highest aspirations and noblest impulses.*

Approximately ten years later, he reformulated his ideal and added this appeal:

The trade unions are the legitimate outgrowth of modern society and industrial conditions. They are not the creation of any man's brain. They are organizations of necessity. They were born of the necessity of the workers to protect and defend themselves from en-

* Pres. Gompers' Report, Convention Proceedings 1889.

17

croachment, injustice and wrong. They are organizations of the working class, for the working class, by the working class; grappling with economic and social problems as they arise, dealing with them in a practical manner to the end that a solution commensurate with the interests of all may be attained. . . . To protect the workers in their inalienable right to a higher and better life; to protect them not only as equals before the law but also in their right to the product of their labor; to protect their lives, their limbs, their health, their homes, their firesides, their liberties as men, workers and citizens; to overcome and conquer prejudice and antagonisms; to secure them the right to life; a right to a full share in the abundance which is the result of their brain and brawn and the civilization of which they are the founders and the main stay; to this the workers are entitled beyond the cavil of a doubt. With nothing less ought they or will they be satisfied. The attainment of these is the glorious mission of the trade unions. No higher or nobler mission ever fell to the lot of a people than that committed to the working class—a class of which we have the honor to be members.*

With this conception of his mission, a few years later he stood across the desk from Theodore Roosevelt and responded to his vehement declaration emphasized by fist pounding "But I am President of the United States of America" with equal fist emphasis and proud assurance "But I am president of the American Federation of Labor."

Samuel Gompers never worked out a blue print of future industry and society. He willingly left to those he considered the "Dreamers" the construction of a new "rainbow" society, and busied himself in evolving road-ways and stepping stones to sustain the feet of thousands and millions pushing onward to life more abundantly. A blueprint, he thought, might distract alert eyes from actual opportunities as they developed. Life often develops differently from what seemed predictable. His eyes were usually on the line of battle.

Inextricably interwoven, Samuel Gompers' thinking and declarations rested on moral law, morality and moral standards. Perhaps this was a by-product of his very early training in the Talmud in the Jewish School of London.

---

*Proceedings Convention American Federation of Labor 1898, President's report.

That training made three powerful principles controlling in his thinking throughout life—moral standards controlling relations with other people, family as the basic unit of society and justice under government by law.

Our movement is based on the justice of Labor's cause. It is economically, socially and morally sound.*

He realized that the nature of its labor movement was of profound importance to the nation and repeatedly said that the spiritual effect of industrial freedom is of incalculable potency in determining the moral fibre of the nation.

Gompers also realized better than most persons in public life that if workers did not use freedom and its opportunities for constructive policies, their alternatives were force, violence and revolution. Either they would develop as a constituent element in a free society with rights and duties or they would oppose existing order to get rights. Rights they must have because they were human beings. He knew many of the leading revolutionaries of his time and learned much from them. Their courage and directness made a powerful appeal to his emotions.

He held that the trade union would and could serve every need of wage-earners. As a business agency, it could take care of their work problems and make for them contracts which determined much of home life. As a social agency, it facilitated participation of workers in community life; as a political agent it could enable workers to share in the making of political policies and decisions; extended to the international field, it would provide labor a voice and influence in relationships and policies in that field; by affording the means for authentic representation it facilitated their participation in various decisions which concerned workers and to which they could contribute information and experience.

After trade unions were functioning as business organizations to attend to the business of wage earners, he expected them to expand their activities to political, social, educational and whatever other fields concerned wage

* 1896 Convention Proceedings, President's Report.

earners. By making the new activity a function of the union instead of forming a separate organization, he strengthened the union, avoided rivalries and conflicting loyalties in labor's welfare and secured economy in administrative costs.

By concentrating power and responsibility in one official, or at least one hierarchy, he limited the danger of organizational rivalries and intrigues. In all probability he never read the Rule of Saint Benedict but evolved from his own experience a basic principle of that rule for monastic life. He wanted the union to conserve its strength and resources for this development:

> Moving step by step, trade unionism contains within itself, as a movement and a mechanism, the possibilities of establishing whatever social institutions the future shall develop for the workers as the predestined universal element in control of society.*

His objectives were broadly to make available to wage earners life more abundantly. He developed as his primary responsibility practical and enduring policies for both immediate gains and future ideals.

He first urged higher wages, shorter hours, safer and better work conditions to provide the necessaries of life so workers could know and use freedom as human beings, to promote their own welfare. At the same time, he sought to strengthen the trade union upon which workers must depend for sustained gains.

As he said,

> It does not require any elaborate social philosophy or great discernment to know a wage of $3.00 a day and a workday of eight hours in a sanitary workshop are better than $2.50 a day and a workday of twelve hours under perilous conditions.*

Upon such issues unions develop solidarity. He expected trade unions would advance from this simple problem to one more complex:

> I believe that wage-earners will continue to become larger sharers per dollar of wealth produced.*

* Convention Proceedings 1910, President's Report.
* Testimony U.S. Commission on Industrial Relations, N.Y. City. May 21–23, 1914.
* Testimony U.S. Industrial Commission April 18, 1899.

3. Union Members

The decision to join the union of his trade, Samuel Gompers held, rested on the right of every individual to personal freedom and freedom of association assured by moral, statutory and constitutional law in the U.S.A. Freedom consists in the utilization by individuals of the opportunities this right affords and association for collective action, when necessary to implement individual choice:

How can a man who is compelled to sell his labor at any price, how can that man be said to have an individuality? Individuality means not simply acting as an individual, but the *power* to act as one, the ability to act as one; having some reserve force by which that individuality can take shape and form to the advantage of its possessor. This has been lost in the modern industrial plants, and it is only by the unity of these individuals, the unity of the working people who have lost their single individuality, that they gain their collective social importance.*

Each worker who wants the power to decide his own life must have the initiative to join with others and as in the case of political government, the people as individuals have ultimate responsibility for the associations:

In connection therewith those early pioneers of the new government saw farther than merely exhausting their energies by making protests which were heard around the world; they coupled with those protests one of the most constructive features of self-government. The central thought was that the destinies of the people of the new nation should be left in the hands of the people themselves.*

In accord with American policies:

Let me tell you just what the Federation is. It is a central labor body bearing the same relation to national and international unions that the Federal Government bears to the states of our Union,

* Address at Fort Edwards, American Federationist, October 1904.
* 1910 Convention Proceedings, President's Report.

21

and the same relation to local unions not identified with national unions that the Federal Government bears to one of our territories.

The local union looks after most of its own affairs just as a municipality of California looks after most of its affairs. Some functions, some powers are reserved for the national and international bodies, however, just as some functions of government are vested in the state rather than in the municipality. In the same way there is a division of authority between the national and international unions and the American Federation of Labor.

Local unions of a given trade are grouped into the State, National and International bodies, which together constitute the Federation.*

He had read and studied the debates, speeches and writings of those American Statesmen of the eighteenth century who wrote the Constitution and initiated the operation of government thereunder. Their principles became his guides to associated action through Federation.

A worker who decides to join a trades union thereby asserts the right to a voice in determining his work life—a development which largely conditions the rest of life for himself and his family. He thereby changes the whole of his living in order to become self-determining. In joining a voluntary organization to advance his own welfare, he exercises his rights as a free individual. The assertion and utilization of such economic rights in no way ignored or minimized duties which rights involved.

Each worker who joins the union of his trade and assumes the obligations of union membership should have one of two elements in his make-up necessary to success in that way of life, said Mr. Gompers:

The first was a thorough knowledge of the trade union movement, its history, its struggles, its tendencies, and for what it stands, or in the absence of this knowledge, that it required absolute faith in the ability of the trade unions to accomplish the amelioration in the condition, and the final emancipation of labor. Talk as one will, but if either one of these two characteristics is not the dominating influence of a trade union leader or member success is an impossibility.*

Mr. Gompers formulated what he considered a defini-

* American Federationist, September 1902.
* American Federationist, January 1895.

tion of a trade unionist in a convention of the cigarmakers international union. After the cigarmakers international union adopted the initiative and referendum, an interval of sixteen years elapsed before a convention of all unions was held. In this interim the organization retrograded losing membership and prestige. Socialists in the unions by using party machinery and finances gained control and manipulated elections and legislative proposals through the initiative and referendum. When the trade unionists succeeded in having a convention held in 1912, debate between trade unionists and Socialist party members was heated and prolonged. Someone asked Mr. Gompers for his definition of a trade unionist. His reply was obviously the result of considered deliberation:

(True trade unionists are) wage-workers, members in good standing of the union of the trade or calling at which they are employed, who realize as a fundamental principle the necessity of unity of all their fellows employed at the same trade or calling; who recognize the vital, logical extension, growth and development of all unions of all trades and callings, and who strive for the unity, federation, cooperation, fraternity, and solidarity of all organized wage-earners; who can and do subordinate self for the common good and always strive for the common uplift; who decline to limit the sphere of their activity by any dogma, doctrine or ism. Finally, those organized wage-workers (are true trade unionists) who fearlessly and insistently maintain and contend that the trade unions, the trade union movement, are paramount to any other form of organization or movement of labor in the world.*

Because Gompers insisted trade unionists must first concentrate on these fundamental objectives which would prepare the way for others, his leadership was characterized by the "intellectual" and other leaders of causes as narrow and materialistic. Insisting that material means to higher standards of living must precede reforms, he antagonized many "liberals," social workers and intellectuals looking for a practical movement to promote programs of reform. His philosophy and his policies early brought him into active conflict with the Socialists, "cheap" money,

* American Federationist, November 1912, p. 905. (Words in parenthesis supplied).

single tax, political organizations, etc. He loved a battle of
wits and used ensuing debates as tactics in educating trade
unionists and solidifying union ranks. One unfortunate result was to lose him the sympathy and cooperation of many
in academic fields. But it was a protection also, for many
who professed sympathy with labor were really primarily
concerned to harness unions to their own special purposes
and objectives.

Mr. Gompers held workers also have the right not
to join unions:

> There may be here and there a worker who for certain reasons
> unexplainable to us does not join a union of labor. This is his right
> no matter how morally wrong he may be. It is his legal right and no
> one can or dare question his exercise of that legal right.*

Samuel Gompers might try to be objective and dispassionate, but he was by nature a partisan. He acknowledged the right of a worker not to belong to a union while
he discounted the decision.

Upon the issue, "Should Socialists who opposed trade
union policies be accepted as members of trade unions,"
he ruled they should be accepted on the same terms as all
other persons but that no political organization as such
could become affiliated.

When the Socialist Party tried to get a foothold within
the A.F. of L. by affiliation of a local unit with the New
York Central Labor Union, Gompers withdrew the Charter
of the N.Y.C.L.U. and ruled that only trade unions were
eligible to membership.

The Socialist side of this continuing controversy was
stated by the New York Call* as follows:

> We Socialists have never pretended either friendship or ad-
> miration for Mr. Gompers and have consistently opposed his policies,
> and though at times we have been acrid and harsh in our treatment
> of him, we have at least been open and candid so that none could
> mistake our meaning. We want Socialist policies substituted for his
> —the recognition of the class struggle, the shifting of the battleground
> largely to the political field, the denial of harmony between labor

---

* Address before Council of Foreign Relations, December 10, 1918,
American Federationist, February 1919.
* December 31, 1912.

and capital, the recognition of the fact by labor there is for it only one side to the industrial problem, to wit, its own.

New York Call was obviously of the same school as present day Pravda.

He urged regular attendance on all union meetings as evidence of concern and evidence of the importance of work. It was the responsibility of members to know what was done in their names.

Though he excused none from responsibility, he repeatedly quoted Herbert Spencer's statement that it has always been the remnant in society that has saved it from reaction and barbarism. While he advocated equality of rights and demanded equality before the law, he never made the mistake of assuming equality of ability:

There is no suspicion in the union doctrine that all men are equal in ability.*

A union he concluded is a practical school:

The work of educating the rank and file of union members in such matters (as affect their interests) has of recent years made much progress ... The primary school in this education is the union meeting. There the members listen to reports of their own committees that deal with such subjects as wages, hours of labor, conditions of employment, unemployment, sickness, industrial accidents, state of the labor market in their respective occupations.* (Words in parenthesis supplied).

Much of our misery as enforced wage-workers springs, not so much from any power exerted by the "upper" or ruling class, as it is the result of the ignorance of so many in our own class who accept conditions by their own volition. . . . The trade unions not only discuss economics and social problems, but deal with them in a practical fashion calculated to bring about better conditions of life to-day, and thus fit the workers for greater struggles for amelioration and emancipation yet to come.*

Gompers was an early advocate of high—then higher—union dues, union benefits, prompt payment of dues and good business administration of union affairs. He did

* Interview, System Magazine, April 1920.
* American Federationist, February 1912.
* Convention Proceedings 1898, President's Report.

much to make "Cheap" policies unpopular and to lead to effective union services.

Trade unionism was to Gompers of the order of religion:

That so long as man shall live and have his being, so long as there shall dwell in the human heart a desire for something better and nobler, so long as there is in the human mind the germ of the belief in human justice and human liberty, so long as there is in the whole makeup of man a desire to be a brother to his fellow-man, so long will there be the labor movement.

It expresses all of the struggles of the past, all the sacrifices and bitterness that the human family has tasted in its experience. The movement embraces all the tenderness of the human family, all of its hopes and all of its aspirations for the real liberty of mankind.

The labor movement is founded on the bedrock of opposition to wrong. It is based on the aspirations for right. I want you, and all of us, to cooperate with the best that is within us to make the labor movement strong and powerful and influential, and that it may grow day by day. And the day that comes shall see for it a better and brighter path than the day that has gone, and open up a new vista of light and life and happiness for the home and fireside and the wife and the children. And that the burden of labor shall be lighter and man shall be a brother to his fellow man.*

* Address Firemen's Convention, August 1904.

4. Union Executives Responsibility

The success of trade unions rests on threefold responsibility—that of the union itself, the union membership and of union executives.

Gompers thus expressed his appreciation of the discipline which performance of official duties gave officers:

A profound and striking social truth is recognized as one's mind dwells on the special and indeed unique schooling to which a representative of labor in the course of his duties is necessarily subjected. He must, if he is to be successful, faithfully interpret the spirit as well as the demands of the members of his union, and in addition he must study the reasoning of the employers in order finally to make the best of his own cause. His views must be at least as broad as the practical labor situation which bears upon his international union, and they ought to be broader, taking in not merely the needs and plans of all organized labor but even in a more remote way all labor. His methods cannot be those of a man who, like the average employer, fights merely for benefits to be enjoyed by a single firm, or company, or locality, or even industry. General principles must be his guide. Business cannot be his foremost care; his concern is human beings. Yet in his method of promoting the aim of his union his business precepts necessarily include system, good faith in keeping contracts, and the general maintenance of financial probity.*

He understood the opportunity for power which the union afforded its executives and cautioned discretion:

We can make of the trade unions exactly what the intelligence and progress of our members will permit. These organizations are of the most elastic character, and whatever action is agreed upon by the organized wage-earning masses can be formulated and achieved by and through the trade unions. It is expected that the leaders of the movement must exercise their best judgment. To artificially and prematurely expand the scope of the organization is to encounter

* American Federationist, November 1910.

27

the danger that the whole fabric may be rent asunder and thus leave all in a plight of misery and despair.*

Responsibility is a necessary quality for intelligent service, he held:

The representative of labor speedily learns responsibility, or else he fails. When through carelessness, or deceit, or instability he has lost a hold upon the employers with whom he has occasion to confer, he quickly finds that he has also undermined his influence with his fellow-union members. The man fully qualified for the position of a labor official dealing with employers has learned to control himself —speaking in conference only when necessary, confining himself to relevant matters, and permitting his opponent to have the questionable satisfaction of uttering opprobrious epithets or bursting into fits of temper.*

He held that experience taught leaders the advantages of avoiding unnecessary conflict.

And let me say to you gentlemen that the officers of an organization of labor who have served any considerable period of time as officers having responsibility that comes from defeat, seek by easy means within their power to avert and avoid contest and conflict. It is not true the charge so often made against the labor leader so called of inciting strikes, contests and conflicts in order, as our opponents put it, to earn their salaries. The men who are most successful in the movements of labor in having the confidence and good will and respect of their fellow workmen are the men who have done the most to avert and avoid strikes. I call your attention to the very well known men of the labor movements of our country for an attestation of that fact and proof of it. I do not pretend to say that here and there you will not find crack-brained, irresponsible and perhaps faithless men; but I do ask you to point to any other vocation and profession of life in which you will not find the same character and quality of men.*

Autocracy has no place in unions, he declared:

There are people in the labor movement who seem to believe that success can only come by entrusting great, yes, absolute power in the hands of an individual or an executive officer. I warn you

* 1892 Convention Proceedings, President's Report.
* American Federationist, November 1910.
* U.S. House Committee on Labor. Testimony, February 11, 1904. Eight Hour Bill on Government Contracts.

against a calamity none greater than which can occur to the labor movement. Autocracy is as dangerous in our movement as in the state. . . . Mistakes may be made by the masses but they learn to do better by reason of their mistakes. The individual, on the contrary, when having absolute power, rarely makes mistakes, rather commits crime. The man who would arrogate to himself in the labor movement absolute and autocratic power would be a tyrant under other circumstances and has no place in the labor movement.*

The primary defense which unions and their members have against usurpation of power by executives is the secret ballot.

All the various union constitutions which Samuel Gompers drafted or helped draft brought executives of the union under regular review by provisions limiting the term of office to one year and by requiring election by vote of members or of their representatives with votes in proportion of membership represented.

He believed officials in the union hierarchy had a responsibility for maintaining discipline and order.

He himself took quick summary action against a high Federation official who violated the non-partisan political policy and that action proved effective in maintaining labor discipline loyal to principles not parties. Thus he supplemented the secret ballot which assured members the right to judge their officials in accord with their own discretion and understanding of American rights.

To safeguard their unions and their rights in and through their unions Samuel Gompers urged the unionists to attend union meetings, accept responsibility for union work and understand what was going on. He repeatedly quoted Junius to remind citizens that rights could be filched from them one by one until freedom was lost and that they should be on the alert to challenge invasion of rights. As he said in 1908:

It is our purpose to see that this country is not alone a haven of civil and religious liberty based upon the spirit of 1776, of 1861, the spirit that made Cuba free as well as the movement that cut the shackles from 4,000,000 black slaves; the spirit of Patrick Henry,

* President's Report, 1888 Convention Proceedings, Page 10.

the spirit of Lincoln. The spirit is not dead and we propose to help in making this country of ours the home of industrial freedom, the three links of civil liberty, religion, equality and opportunity and industrial freedom, and under God's guidance moving onward and forward accomplishing the dream of the poet—the brotherhood of man.*

Trade unions, through their leaders, have been persistent and effective in registering protests against wrongs and have led to wider justice.

Gompers himself kept in touch with happenings in local trade unions by his habit of talking with rank and file union members all over the country and he urged other union executives to do the same. He was never accused of ceasing to be a working man. He spotted those with outstanding ability and discussed with them problems and proposals—a practice which often disclosed hidden difficulties. By studying experience—not books—he detected trends and future difficulties and anticipated need for principles and policies for action. He had strongly developed intuitions that enabled him to feel men's thinking and draw upon the past experience of various groups.

He warned union executives against evading the right of union membership to determine goals.

The goals of a union should be determined only by its members, he warned:

Wage earners have a right to inaugurate a revolution if they think such action is justified but no leaders have a right to involve workers in revolutions under guise of a strike. A strike is something very different from a revolution. A strike is for the purpose of gaining some definite, concrete improvement in working conditions. . . . If a strike results in tangible benefits, those benefits are definitely formulated in the agreement by which the contest ends and industrial peace is restored.*

Now and then Mr. Gompers referred to early experience which taught him the value of moderation in language. Samuel Gompers had a powerful emotional temperament and in his early days fiery proposals made a strong appeal to him. He told how Karl Laurrell would

---

* Address, Chicago, May 1, 1908.
* American Federationist, November 1916.

start him in discussion, lead him on by questions and encourage him by concentrated attention and then when he had finished Laurrell would turn on him the power of a strong clear mind with a store of practical experience that would completely refute his arguments and with emotions coldly controlled, demolish his emotional contentions. It was good training in resilience and in learning to take criticism for mistakes. An experience exposing the danger of emotional leadership he never forgot.

In an effort to get state action for relief of the unemployed during the major depression of 1893, Mr. Gompers suggested a demonstration and mass meeting in Madison Square Garden. He felt the situation was a blight on our "boasted intelligence and civilization." In speaking to that meeting, he poured out the bitterness of his soul against making workers suffer the misery and degradation of unemployment and roused his own passion and that of the mass audience using all his dramatic abilities to express their wrongs. He had his audience on their feet shouting, cheering and awaiting his direction. Badly frightened at what he had aroused, he turned all his abilities to bringing his audience back to safety and he resolved never again to give free rein to his emotions.

The story of his ceaseless journeying throughout the length and breadth of the land wherever there was trouble in work-a-day lives, and wherever there was need for his help, is the record of the building of the American labor movement. When the "Chief", as they called him, appeared they told him their troubles, confident he would understand. He gave them counsel and often help and reinforcements wherever he went. He talked with local union members and so kept close to local union operations from which trends and new movements developed. It also gave him personal contacts with an incredibly large number of wage earners. This knowledge in many ways enabled him to aid in advancing those who showed understanding and constructive capacities. The labor movement he led was an army of wage earners brought together by common problems and interests and held together by mutual needs and purposes and common ideals.

5. Contract-Participation in Our Market Economy

Workers who assume responsibility for directing their work lives by joining a union, elect union officers who become their agents in business relations. A main function of these agents is the negotiation of contracts with employers which fix terms and conditions under which service is performed. Use of contracts—the essence of which is mutuality—is the workers' next important discipline for the free way of life. Performance of specific service is not enforceable but damages due to failing to perform services may be had through legal means. Compulsory service except in penal institutions is incompatible with human freedom.

S. G.'s personal experience with contract negotiations was limited to his early career as an officer of his cigarmakers union and as titular president of the Federation's federal trade and labor unions.

Responsibility for contract negotiation lay with the national and international unions which had autonomy or self-government within their economic jurisdictions prescribed by the Federation. The Federation had responsibility for over-all policies and served as a clearance agency for union experience and progress.

In order to give contract negotiation the dependability and the dignity necessary for permanence in addition to the morality involved, Samuel Gompers insisted upon scrupulous fulfillment of all contracts. Only violation of such contracts by employers could release unions from their obligation.

Two facts should be emphasized. One, that it is the aim and purpose of the organized labor movement of our country to have employers and workmen faithfully carry out the terms of an agree-

32

ment or contract in regard to labor and the conditions of employment. The other is that such an agreement or contract is not specifically enforceable by employers or by workmen.

In all the land there is no law by which any one is bound to specifically perform the service specified in any agreement or contract.*

The American Federation of Labor has repeatedly declared and emphasized the principle that agreements entered into between organized workmen and their employers covering a specific period, with provisions for wages, hours, and conditions of employment, should be sacredly kept.*

With pride he gave this public testimony of how unions enforce the keeping of contracts and thus maintain a structure of economic government responsible for relations between management and workers, "resting on mutuality of interests, dependability, practicability, confidence and good faith":

You do not know what it means for a man in his national or international trade union to rise up and say: "You shall not and dare not, within the confines and under the jurisdiction of this international union, pursue the course you have; and unless you return to work within an hour or twenty-four hours, as the case may be, your charter, your affiliation to this international union, part of the American Federation of Labor, shall be severed and severed at once." Men in the American labor movement have that courage to say those things, and they do it. They have done it. They have done it within the past few days in three instances of my personal knowledge.*

For the laggards he recommended only the compulsion of facts and moral obligation:

Non-unionists who reap the rewards of union effort, without contributing a dollar or risking a loss of a day, are parasites. They are reaping a benefit from the union spirit, while they themselves are debasing genuine manhood. Having rights, they are too cowardly to stand up for them—the right of being one of the parties to a two-party contract; the right to take a share in the world-wide struggle of labor for the advance of the working classes; the right to speak

* American Federationist, August 1912.
* From testimony before U.S. Commission on Industrial Relations, New York City, May 21–23, 1914.
* Address, National Industrial Conference, Washington, D.C., October 17, 1919.

up for labor, before the employer, before the public, before the lawgivers, before the oppressors of working women and children. What would become of the general movement for factory and mine inspection, safety appliances in regard to machinery, for enforcing labor bureau laws, for compensation in case of injuries, for increasing the age when children may go to work, the limitation of the hours of labor, etc., etc., were it not for the trade unions? Every non-union employee knows the truth which such questions must evoke in reply. The consequence must be, and sooner or later always is, that the still, small voice of honor, working without cease and secretly in each man's mind and heart, causes him to yearn for the fellowship of the men of courage gathered together in the unions, and finally impels him to seize the occasion to break away from his feudal relations with his employer and convert the latter from a master into a fellow-creature who is in the market to buy something from his equal—the man who sells his labor power.*

Since unions obligated themselves to the fulfillment of specific terms and conditions they needed control over all workers affected. For this reason they developed the practice of writing into contracts union-shop provisions—that is, they either would supply workers as needed with the experience and the competence required for the work or all non-members hired should have a limited period of work after which they should join the union and fulfill union obligations.

He held that the union shop was not closed:

Recently the opponents of organized labor started an agitation for what they euphoniously designate as the "open shop"; and several employers, otherwise fair, having been persuaded that the proposition on the surface appears to be ethical, have advocated it. On the other hand, our movement stands for the union shop, not, as our opponents designate it, the closed shop; for, as a matter of fact, a union shop is not a closed shop. Any wage-earner, a member of an organization in any part of the country, can enter the union shop. And any wage-earner, competent to fill any position in the union shop, is not only eligible to enter to work therein, but the organizations have their hundreds of missionaries at work, in and out of season, urging and pleading with them to enter the wide-open doors of the union. This so-called open shop is the disintegrating factor that leads to the non-union shop; in other words, the shop which is closed to the

* American Federationist, June 1910.

union man, no matter from whence he hails or what his skill and competency. . . .

Agreements or joint bargains of organized labor with employers depend for their success upon the good will of the union and the employers toward each other. Neither should be subject to the irresponsibilty or lack of intelligence of the non-unionist, or his failure to act in concert with, and bear the equal responsibility of, the unionist. Hence, the so-called open shop makes agreements and joint bargains with employers impracticable, if not impossible. The union can not be responsible for non-unionists whose conduct often renders the terms of the agreement ineffective and nugatory.*

The union shop rests on the freedom of contract, or individual liberty. There is no greater element of "monopoly" in it than in any other contract for services or materials.*

Organized labor's insistence upon and work for, not the "closed-shop," as our opponents term it, but the union shop, in agreement with employers, mutually entered into for the advantage of both and the maintenance of industrial peace with equity and justice for both, is to the economic, social and moral advancement of all our people.

The union shop, in agreement with employers, is the application of the principle that those who enjoy the benefits and advantages resulting from an agreement shall also equally bear the moral and financial responsibilities involved.*

Contracts as they develop to prescribe for various problems and conditions set up an economic order corresponding to social order through political government.

* President's report, 1903 Convention Proceedings.
* American Federationist, October 1904.
* President's report, 1905 Convention Proceedings.

6. Pure and Simple Trade Unionism

"Pure and simple" trade unionism meant economic power organized in an effective association of persons with similar needs and goals, directed for an objective, immediate and practical. Results in higher wages, shorter hours, and opportunities for justice strengthened forces binding the group together. Union discipline held the weaker members in line. Strong, intelligent, devoted leaders were indispensable. Samuel Gompers and his group by example and by precept inculcated the guiding moral principles and stimulated an understanding spirit and will that sustained leaders and members for hardships and endurance. Trade unionism was to them a way of life.

All workers with paid-up trade union cards should be accepted by similar unions and accorded equal rights with all others. Some were members of the Socialist Party, devoted to its tenets. Their speeches and proposals afforded the "pure and simple" advocates opportunity to explain why they believed Socialism wrong and why they believed economic remedies for economic problems more effective. More were members of the Democratic or the Republican party. Party membership was not a union concern.

To keep the American Federation of Labor an organization of workers, by workers, for workers, the American Federation of Labor gathered under its aegis wage-earners with common work interests and needs. It denied a charter to a powerful Central Labor Union in New York City which had permitted a local unit of the Socialist Labor Party to affiliate. It would have taken the same action in case the local unit had belonged to any other political party. Blocked in their policy of infiltration, the Socialist Labor Party then built up the Socialist Trades and Labor Alliance, a dual labor organization, which was opposed and defeated with all the emotional bitterness which attends fra-

36

tricidal or civil wars. Mr. Gompers and his "pure and simple" fellow workers were villified and abused in public speeches and the Socialist press. Later other labor organizations with revolutionary, conflicting philosophy and purposes were launched as rivals and bitterly opposed: The American Labor Union, and the Industrial Workers of the World, etc.

Workers united in "pure and simple" trade unions to solve their economic problems. Political and religious preferences were matters for individual, not group decision and not proper subjects for Federation deliberation or for its regional and local bodies.

The "pure and simple" aimed at control and use of unions in accord with the wishes of their members and not control over management, industry, political parties or government.

In his report to the Detroit Convention, 1890, Mr. Gompers included these paragraphs:

... The conviction is deeply rooted in me that in the trade union movement the first condition requisite is good-standing membership in a trade union, regardless of to which party a man might belong.

Those who have had any experience in the labor movement will admit the great work and forbearance, tact and judgment requisite to maintain harmony in organization. The trade unions are no exception to this rule. In the trade union movement I have ever endeavored to attain that much-desired end, and recognize that that in itself is of a sufficiently important nature and requirement as to preclude the possibility of jointly acting with organizations based upon different practical workings or policy.

I am willing to subordinate my opinions to the well-being, harmony and success of the labor movement; I am willing to sacrifice myself also in the furtherance of any action it may take for its advancement; I am willing to step aside if that will promote our cause, but I can not and will not prove false to my convictions that the trade unions pure and simple are the natural organizations of the wage-workers to secure their present material and practical improvement and to achieve their final emancipation.*

As a result of Samuel Gompers' successful enforcement of policies of pure and simple trade unionism a number of

* President's report, Convention Proceedings, 1890.

circumstances enabled the Socialists to defeat him for re-election as President in 1894. Mr. Gompers believed the two most important were: The presence of John Burns, English Socialist, at the convention, and the bankruptcy of the Miner's Union which made its president, John Mc-Bride, available.

Membership in the trade union, Gompers held, should be controlled by eligibility to work on the job over which the particular national craft union had jurisdiction and by a paid-up union card. No union had a right to question to what political party, church, lodge or sect he belonged. Gompers further held that these relationships were not proper matters for discussion or decision in trade unions. The union's function was to mobilize workers for collective action to attain common economic and work purposes and mutual welfare. Partisan political action, religion, membership in other private associations were matters for individual preference and action, he held. To bring such matters into union meeting meant bringing in causes of division—not unity.

By restricting action to obtainable objectives upon which there was unity, progress was made which stimulated further growth:

The American Federation of Labor is a movement that instils confidence and hope because it is founded upon continual achievements. It does not hold out inflated hopes and impossible ideals which must collapse and disappear before real industrial problems and attacks. The insistent and consistent policy of the trade union movement has secured for the working people whatever of uplift and betterment has made their lives freer and happier. This policy has been one of uncompromising protest and agitation against every form of wrong, injustice, or denial of rights. In the economic field this policy has resulted in effective and triumphant contest. It has inspired workers with the desire, the purpose and the grit to struggle and battle for material improvement in the form of higher wages, fewer hours of labor, better conditions of employment. In the political field the policy has been to avoid alliance with any political party, but to utilize all parties, whenever an opportunity is presented to remedy wrong or inaugurate new and better policies in legislation, administration, or judicature. The American Federation of Labor has always been maintained untrammeled, unrestricted, free to criticize, attack or denounce men, employers, parties, whenever the welfare and the interests of the workers have been menaced.*

The ground-work principle of America's labor movement has been to recognize that first things must come first. The primary essential in our mission has been the protection of the wage-worker, now; to increase his wages; to cut hours off the long workday, which was killing him; to improve the safety and the sanitary conditions of the workshop; to free him from the tyrannies, petty and otherwise, which served to make his existence a slavery. These, in the nature of things, I repeat, were and are the primary objects of trade unionism.

Our great Federation has uniformly refused to surrender this conviction and to rush to the support of any one of the numerous society-saving or society-destroying schemes which decade by decade have been sprung upon this country. A score of such schemes, having a national scope, and being for the passing day subject to popular discussion, have gone down behind the horizon and are now but ancient history. But while our Federation has thus been conservative, it has ever had its face turned toward whatever reforms, in politics or economics, could be of direct and obvious benefit to the working classes. It has never given up its birthright for a mess of pottage. It has pursued its avowed policy with the conviction that if the lesser and immediate demands of labor could not be obtained now from society as it is, it would be mere dreaming to preach and pursue that will-o'-the-wisp, a new society constructed from rainbow materials—a system of society on which even the dreamers themselves have never agreed.*

In improving conditions from day to day the organized labor movement has no "fixed program" for human progress. If you start out with a program everything must conform to it. With theorists, if facts do not conform to their theories, then so much the worse for the facts. Their declarations of theories and actions refuse to be hampered by facts. We do not set any particular standard, but work for the best possible conditions immediately obtainable for the workers. When they are obtained then we strive for better. . . .

The working people will not stop when any particular point is reached; they will never stop in their efforts to obtain a better life for themselves, for their wives, for their children, and for all humanity. The object is to obtain complete social justice.*

* American Federationist, July 1913.
* From President's report, Convention Proceedings, 1911.
* From abstract of testimony before United States Commission on Industrial Relations, New York City, May 21–23, 1914.

American Federation of Labor is a progressive movement, not revolutionary, he reiterated again and again:

The trade union movement is a progressive movement to
secure some of the advantages which have come by reason of the
great production of wealth; to secure a normal workday; to secure
a wage that shall bring comfort into the home, that shall afford
an opportunity to the workers to give advantages to their children
and their dependents, that these children may have the opportunity
of going to the schools, the colleges and the universities; that they
may be taken out of the factories, the work-shops, the mills and
the mines and given an opportunity to run, to play in God's sunshine, and that they may grow up into the manhood and the woman-
hood of the future upon which our Republic and our institutions
depend.

The American labor movement is not at war with society.
It seeks to overthrow nothing. It is as loyal and devoted to the
ideals of our Republic as any group or individual in all America
can be. And it is not fair to the men and the women in the American
labor movement to attempt now to place them in the position of
disloyalty or failure to appreciate and to give service to this ideal
of the world's government, the Republic of the United States of
America.*

Samuel Gompers held the first duty of the American
Federation of Labor was to organize unions and then to
teach them how to use their economic power.

As he frequently pointed out wage-earners wanted
two objectives which progressively brought betterment in
their lives—higher wages which made possible higher living standards in their homes and wider opportunities and
fewer work hours which gave them leisure for recuperation
of vitality, for pleasure and study and home life together
with opportunity to join in normal community life. These
were revolutionizing changes which led to constructive development for individuals in their communities. They represented the practical statesmanship of a leader who
grasped the importance of continuity in human institutions
and who realized material progress could facilitate the
purposes of spiritual forces. They also represented the experience of a leader who curbed his impatience so as to

* Address, Boston Chamber of Commerce, 1920.

lead one step at a time, instilling into his followers a goal to be achieved without destroying the benefits they had. Instinctively he urged procedures that accustomed trade unionists to principles of conservatism. His ridicule of the socialist-communist methods and program cleared the way for constructive thinking and appreciation of orderly planning. He taught directly and indirectly that the true radical and the useful revolutionary not only sought justice, but understood that justice could result from the proper functioning of available institutions and that each individual had a responsibility for that proper functioning.

Personally he was no weakling and did not seem to know what fear was. When his advice to use and maintain rights involved travelling a pathway with personal discomforts and dangers, he led the way even when it led to jail.

So his policy of pure and simple trade unionism which seemed slow, narrow and unstimulating to some workers, Socialists and intellectuals, was his method of mobilizing and disciplining workers in sufficient numbers so that they might have economic power adequate for solving their problems and might use it for practical purposes that would grow into power for even larger goals and more inclusive programs. As he told the 1912 Convention, "We do need new devices and new methods of political expression, but not half so much as we need to realize and to use the power we now have and to consecrate ourselves and our ability to humanity's cause." By limiting the number of projects he made it practical to press harder on those chosen—for "more, more and then more" and lay the foundations for more projects.

Strengthening and extending the trade union structure was partly the responsibility of national trade unions and partly of the Federation. The Federation concentrated on unorganized areas. With funds quite inadequate in the early years even for the central office, Mr. Gompers had to depend on volunteer helpers. He devised a commission which gave these organizers an official status and selected persons he knew to be loyal to trade union principles and willing to give themselves and their leisure. These volunteer organizers helped to stimulate in the growing Federation a spirit of local self reliance as well as appreciation of tangible, practical returns in terms of better conditions of work, higher wages, shorter hours and machinery for adjusting disputes and new problems. Understanding of what a union could do and responsibility for getting results from it, instilled in local leadership and union members, is what has given the American Federation of Labor vitality, endurance and flexibility. The traditions of voluntarism have been preserved at the base of the structure.

7. Collective Bargaining

As wage-earners organized in trade unions to use their economic power to promote their own welfare, they moved from status to contract in our economy and became self-directing influential components of industries. Unions elect representatives to negotiate contracts stipulating terms and conditions of work.

The terms and conditions under which production workers give services in industry should be matters of contract between the parties concerned as are all other matters of business. It is hard to realize now what a difficult achievement it was to initiate this procedure in the early days when employers assumed that these conditions were matters for them as owners to determine.

The extension and development of union contracts became the key to progress for labor.

As each national and international union has exclusive control over contract negotiations, Mr. Gompers' statements are for the most part confined to general principles controlling improved conditions of employment—wages and hour standards.

WAGES

Samuel Gompers and his trade unions did not believe that "economic iron law" determined the wage rates and hours of work for wage earners but on the contrary, workers, management and market demands conditioned output, costs of production, quality of output and prices, sales, profits, compensation of the production force, etc. For wage earners, compensation included two basic elements—hours of work and rates of pay. Wage and hour standards control and condition the whole of the wage-earners' lives—in the work places, their homes and their communities. Negotiation of these standards has been attended by sharp

43

and prolonged contentions, and development of union theory and principles. He early learned wages are determined by people not laws:

> Increases in the number of workers do not lead to lower rates —increased productivity, improved processes and machinery, cheaper operating power, improved managerial methods, increased demand, and innumerable other modifying variables may tend to maintain the wage-level, or to raise it. But, perhaps, the most potent factor of all in raising wage-levels is the combined and determined efforts of the workers themselves . . .
>
> Without introducing any other new factor into the situation, if the employees of an industry paying extremely low wages are organized, wages may by collective action be repeatedly raised. Innumerable permutations and adjustments make this increase possible. That a limit is set to this increase by the marginal productivity of the laborer is generally and historically accurate. The worker who can make one shoe a day may feel perfectly sure that this productive limit will effectually bar him from receiving as wages the value of two shoes, but he may not feel at all sure it will guarantee wages commensurate with the value of the productive labor he put into the one shoe he did produce. Added to productive efficiency must be effectiveness in making wage demands. But to say that each employer knows the productivity per workman, not to mention the marginal productivity in the industry, is an absurdly preposterous claim. Wages are for the most part paid on the trial and balance principle, fixing them as low as the workman will stand and not according to any rational, well-formulated theory. That is to say, the distributive share allotted to the wage-earners is the result of human activity, either of the employers or the employees, and not the normal or inevitable result of any natural law.*

S. G. taught unions that wages were payment for work done and at the same time a factor in costs of production and in national income which sustained retail markets. Through contract negotiation they learned to use economic law and principles to promote their own interests.

In 1898, Samuel Gompers thus defined a living wage:

> A minimum wage—a living wage which, when expended in the most economical manner, shall be sufficient to maintain an average-sized family in a manner consistent with whatever the contemporary local civilization recognizes as indispensable to physical

---

* American Federationist, July 1913.

and mental health, or as required by the rational self-respect of human beings.*

After experiencing the economic depressions which followed the business recession beginning in 1873, the panic of 1893, and watching the cumulative effect of wage cuts initiated by employers in 1903 and again in 1907, Samuel Gompers sent practical warning and directive rousing all wage-earner groups like a fiery cross:

We have advised and shall continue to advise our fellow-workmen to resist reductions in wages by every lawful means within their power, for as we have said before, "It is better to resist and lose than not to resist at all."

Let workmen complacently accept reductions in their wages and it will be an invitation to repeat the reduction at will, intensifying the depression and provoking an industrial crisis; forcing down the workers in the economic and social scale and bringing on fearful poverty, misery and degradation. Resistance on the part of labor to reduction of wages will check this to a great degree and at least demonstrate to the ignorant and short-sighted employers that such a course is exceedingly expensive to them, and will prevent its repetition.*

He delighted to tell how unorganized as well as organized workers followed his leadership and how J. P. Morgan, then at the height of his power, in an interview announced that the interests he represented would not reduce wages.

The entire history of industry demonstrates clearly beyond question that every effort in the past to reduce wages, every reduction of wages made to relieve a like situation, has simply accentuated and made the condition worse. It is the largest possible consumption of things produced which makes the largest possible prosperity and I may say this, without further attempt at serious argument—I may say this, that the *employers of labor who make or believe they can make an attempt to force wages down are not going to have the easy sailing they had years ago*, for the American workmen have come to the conclusion that if for any reason—and I shall not attempt to assign one tonight—the financial situation is as it is, it is due to no fault of theirs; that whoever is to blame,

* American Federationist, April 1898. Article in reply to Edward Atkinson, on minimum living wage.
* American Federationist, January 1904.

it is in the hands of the financiers or the captains of industry and the representatives in Congress, if you please, if you care to blame them; but I repeat, it is not due to any fault of the working people. They have made up their minds that they are not going to be the chief sufferers either by reason of an artificially made panic or by the blunders of those who have the affairs of finance and industry under their direction.*

He argued high wages do not necessarily cause high prices but may help to lower them:

It is said that requests for increases in wages necessitate increases in prices, which increase cost of living and in return result in more wage demands—a vicious circle that leads to no progress. It should be remembered that wages constitute only one of the factors in production costs and that high-wage labor invariably leads to labor saving machinery and improved production processes. High wages do not inevitably lead to the vicious circle. On the contrary, they have invariably resulted in constructive changes, beneficial to workers and resulting in increased production.*

He opposed fixing by law minimum wages or maximum hours in private employment even for women:

When the question of fixing, by legal enactment, minimum wages for women was before the Executive Council of the American Federation of Labor for investigation and discussion, and subsequently before the convention of the American Federation of Labor, there was a great diversion of views. I am betraying no confidence when I say that. The official decision of the convention was that the subject was worthy of further discussion and consideration. In my judgment the proposal to establish by law a minimum wage for women, though well meant, is a curb upon the rights, the natural development, and the opportunity for development of the women employed in the industries of our country.

. . . I am very suspicious of the activities of governmental agencies. I apprehend that once the state is allowed to fix a minimum rate, the state would also take the right to compel men or women to work at that rate. I have some apprehension that if the legislature were allowed to establish a maximum workday it might also compel workmen to work up to the maximum allowed.*

* American Federationist, February 1908.
* Address convention of Associated Advertising Clubs of the World, New Orleans, September 22, 1919.
* Testimony, U.S. Commission on Industrial Relations, New York City, May 21–23, 1914.

S. G. was among the first to point out there must be a balance between purchasing power and production and the share of purchasing power going to wages:

The merchant, no matter of what class, depends largely on the volume of purchases made by wage earners every week for food, clothing, household goods and even many things not classed as absolute necessities. The more freely such purchases are made the greater the volume of money kept in circulation. The amount of furniture, for instance, which is purchased all over the country in a month is the regulator of how much furniture the factories will produce. The same argument applies to all other commodities necessary for civilized existence.

It must be remembered that while the individual purchases of the wealthy are often striking in amount, yet the great volume of trade in everything that pertains to living comes from the masses of the people—those on wages or salary.*

One of the functions of organized labor is to increase the share of the workers in the product of their labor.*

Wages—the workers' share of returns from production—should be restricted only by industrial success:

When a number of associated persons may freely decide as to whether they shall work or not, and uphold that decision, they have in their hands the economic power to secure to themselves from the products of industry a share restricted only by industrial success.*

SHORTER WORKDAY

The shorter eight-hour workday in Gompers' time schedule of action took precedence over wage increases:

The general reduction of the hours of labor to eight per day would reach further than any other reformatory measure; it would be of more lasting benefit; it would create a greater spirit in the working man; it would make him a better citizen, a better father, a better husband, a better man in general.*

In 1886 as president of the American Federation of Labor he initiated the industry-wide eight-hour movement

* Journal of Commerce article, December 27, 1907.
* American Federationist, August 1914, page 621.
* President's report, Convention Proceedings, 1910.
* Testimony, United States Senate Committee upon the Relations Between Labor and Capital, (Henry W. Blair, chairman), 1883.

for that standard through collective bargaining. In that year the Cigarmakers were generally successful in establishing eight-hours throughout their industry. In 1890 another industry-wide movement for eight-hours was led by the Carpenters and S. G. reported success "throughout the whole country," with benefit to nearly all trades and callings.

In the next general campaign the miners were selected to head the movement. The miners were having internal difficulties so at the last minute S. G. sent an emissary to Europe to invite a few unions there to start a similar movement on May 1.

After these shorter-hours movements, the Federation under Samuel Gompers generally left this field to collective bargaining under the leadership of national and international unions. He frequently justified the results of their policies by compiling union statistics to show the resulting better health and longer lives.

Enforcement of the Federal eight-hour law covering government workers and those working under Federal contracts was one of the early demands of the Federation. S. G. consistently opposed law for the establishment or maintenance of the eight-hour day in private industry. His last big battle against "eight hours by law" was against a resolution in the 1915 San Francisco convention. He won and he continued his educational opposition throughout the year. In a pamphlet issued during the year he pointed out these difficulties:

The mere enactment of eight-hour legislation would not decrease one iota the necessity for economic organization and the economic struggle. Indeed, instead of helping, it only adds another obstacle to the achievement of a real, general eight-hour day. Instead of employees dealing directly with their employers, it would be necessary for the organizations to use their influence upon lawmakers to secure the enactment of an eight-hour law in all private industries and occupations, and then continue to use their influence even more remote and indirect upon the administrative agents whose duty it would be to enforce the law, and again, whatever influence they might have still more remote and indirect, in securing an understanding and a favorable interpretation of the eight-hour law by the judiciary. Who knows but that by judicial interpretation and enforcement an eight-hour law would work to the undoing of labor's fight of ages for freedom?*

He advocated also shortening the work week to the five and a half day week and holidays with pay.

UNION-MANAGEMENT COOPERATION

S. G. foresaw cooperation between management and unions through collective bargaining arrangements to reduce seasonal lay-offs:

It (seasonal work) demoralizes both employer and employee. The employer gets in the habit of shutting down the moment that sufficient work is not afforded and the employee is continuously harassed by a feeling of uncertainty and is easily led away into the delusion that by soldiering on his job he can prolong it. Here is a point in which the interests of the employer and the employee are not in conflict and where their best brains can well be pooled to take advice with production engineers for the planning of the work in such a way as to avoid slack seasons.

It will develop that both profits and wages are too low because of the excessive waste of seasonal business. If capital and labor will only cooperate to war upon waste they will both find it far more profitable than warring upon one another.*

* American Federationist, March 1916.
* Interview of Samuel Crowther with Samuel Gompers, System Magazine, April 1920.

8. Unions and Employers

Mr. Gompers at no time advocated that wage-earners assume functions that belonged to management and owners. As he phrased it:

> When workmen insist upon certain terms, they are not seeking to control the employer's business but to lay down the conditions of their own participation in that business.*

Samuel Gompers did not seek to advance workers by taking rights from employers. In an address made in Chicago in 1908, he declared with considerable fervor:

> The wealth possessors are free wherever they go, and I will not begrudge them their freedom. All we insist upon is being free ourselves. There is no power or factor so potent to maintain the freedom that we now possess, and to obtain absolute equality before the law and equality of opportunity as the labor organizations of our time.*

As to business combinations he said:

> I will not join—I have not joined—in that hue and cry against combinations of capital. I realize that that is a matter of economy and development and strength.
>
> But I do say, and I might say it parenthetically, that I object to the organizations of capital popularly known as "trusts," when they attempt to interfere with the political affairs of our country, and particularly the judiciary. I am speaking of them from an industrial and not from a commercial point of view.*
>
> Organized labor understands that there is organization in capital and among capitalists. You will have to look in another direction for denunciations of the organization of capital than in the annals and the records of organized labor. Our movement re-

---

* American Federationist, July 1902.
* Address, Chicago, May 1, 1908.
* Address, National Civic Federation, New York City. American Federationist, February 1902.

gards the organization of capital as the association of our employers. They are as good or bad as they are good or bad employers, and the organization *per se* is not the thing which is either good or bad.*

He explained the bases of cooperation between workers and management thus:

I admit that our trade union movement is not perfect, but I submit that there is not a single voluntary organization in this or any other country which has contributed so much to a constructive policy within rational lines. The declaration which we have proposed is rejected and repudiated by the employing group. They want shop organizations, the employers' union. They are building upon quicksand. They are resting their hope upon flimsy ground, in their benevolent and solicitous attitude toward the workers in their employ. An organization means something. It means that any group of workers shall have the free opportunity to express themselves, and that in the course of time and experience they will become, as every labor organization in America and throughout the world has become, more considerate and under the obligation of duty and responsibility . . .

If the workers maintain their organization, time makes them realize their responsibility, and the employers experience a change in the mental attitude that they are masters of all they survey, and sit down and discuss in conference means and methods by which these adjustments and agreements and collective bargaining are brought about.*

As fair distribution of shares in returns from production he recommended:

The full value of production does not go to the actual workingmen today. A portion goes to investment, superintendence, agencies for the creation of wants among people, and many other things. Some of these are legitimate factors in industry entitled to reward, but many of them should be eliminated. The legitimate factors are superintendency, the creation of wants, administration, returns for investment insofar as it is honest investment and does not include watered stock or inflated holdings.*

The proportions to which the "creation of wants" has

* Address, Buffalo, January 9, 1903.
* Address, National Industrial Conference, Washington, D.C., October 22, 1919.
* United States Commission on Industrial Relations, New York City, May 21–23, 1914.

gone were not foreseeable in Mr. Gompers' time or he probably would have modified the legitimacy of this factor's share in returns as he did that of investment.

Throughout his long career as union leader Samuel Gompers never lost sight of the consequences of the alternative to constructive and conservative trade unionism. In 1893 in that winter of terrible unemployment, the American Federation of Labor convention met in the City Hall in Chicago and its delegates daily passed through the stone corridor where homeless destitute men slept on the floor and on steps. He issued a warning out of deep emotion:

> The path of the progress of organized labor has been strewn with the unmarked graves of heroes and heroines. . . . Through the dark ages of man's development to the present day organized labor stands for hope, humanity and progress. To it credit is due that we today see clearer the wrongs and injustices which prevail. It voices the hopes of the future and calls to account those responsible for the present. Last night I walked through the corridors of the City Hall and saw hundreds of men lying on the stone flooring, on the iron steps and some asleep standing up—all men in enforced idleness. Those responsible for these conditions should take warning. They are sleeping in false security.
>
> The men responsible for these things, who send out their protests, in which we join, against the bomb in Barcelona, against the bomb in Paris, and against the assassin's bullet in Chicago must understand they must concede to the solution of the problem that organized labor presents or they will be confronted with the guerilla warfare to which I have alluded. Organized labor presents a solution of these problems. I appeal to those responsible men because the responsibility is resting on their shoulders. If they oppose organized labor in its solution of these questions, the people, without assembling, unbridled, unanswerable and irresponsible, may—but who can foretell what dangers may confront the human family? If, on the other hand, those responsible for these conditions will take the advice of the friends of humanity before it is too late, conditions may be reversed, and a prosperous and just and human condition reinstated.*

About two decades later as a war-time railway strike lay in the balance awaiting railway executives' decision, discouraging information came over the telephone. He sat

* Convention Proceedings, 1893, page 9.

back in reflection and said to himself: "If it should come and I should have to take charge will I have the wisdom?"

The old revolutionary spirit was not dead but was held under a tight leash.

While his early years of leadership were dominated by bitter and merciless fighting and contest between management and workers, in later years he caught a vision of the possibilities of cooperation and had the viability to welcome it. He appreciated the achievements of the great "Captains of Industry" but also sensed at what great wastes and costs!

He rejected government ownership and control as an alternative to economic order:

As a matter of fact, conditions in Australia lead to the conviction that governmental ownership and control solve nothing. They simply transfer industrial problems to the political field, restate them in political terms and then try to solve them by political methods. They do not touch the causes of industrial unrest as directly and as effectively as the use of economic agencies and methods. The industrial injustice resultant from the evils in modern industry as well as the result of the inherent weakness and characteristics of human nature has not been bettered but made infinitely worse by government ownership and control. These fundamental causal elements can best be held in check by the stronger economic force, at least until social and individual morality reach a higher plane.*

He early sensed the development of a new despotism—dictatorship by bureaucrats:

Government ownership and control like other institutions grow by what they feed on. Government ownership and control instituted for one phase of industrial relations gradually but inevitably reach out to other connected relations until the whole is under the domination not of the people but of an oligarchy—a bureaucracy.

A good illustration of immediate conditions resulting from putting all forces and institutions at the service of society exists today in Germany. There is no consideration given the individual, the welfare of the majority is the declared purpose of every policy. All of the activities, the relations and the customs of the nation are specifically regulated in the interest of the nation. What is a war measure there constitutes the negation of personal freedom. Each individual is assigned to that work by which he can contribute the

* American Federationist, June 1915.

greatest service to the majority of the people. Everything is controlled—the use of the land for agriculture and the number of slices of bread. The regulation is efficient.*

Policies for government employees and basic safeguards of their human rights may be modified by changing conditions. When government entered the field of business enterprise and performed functions other than government, Gompers held that employees in such work also needed union organizations to establish and conduct contractual relations through which to reach mutually satisfactory standards. The appropriate craft unions were expected to serve. He held that all government employees had the right to organize and to exercise fundamental constitutional rights—and must rely upon legislation for higher standards. Only those in non-governmental enterprise have the right to strike and rely upon collective bargaining. In the following statement Mr. Gompers indicates it might be necessary to reconsider denial of the right of government workers to strike under all circumstances, even though he did not foresee the present extent to which Big Government has invaded and dominated Big Business and to which Big Business has invaded Big Government.

The employees of the government are denied the right collectively to lay down their tools or implements of their work and quit. They cannot strike. They are forbidden to strike. A few letter carriers in West Virginia a few months ago undertook collectively to send in their resignations. They have been indicted and in order that they might have the smallest, lowest sentences imposed upon them, some of them consented, under protest, and did plead guilty and thus the precedent has been established. How it was brought about, how it was manipulated, I am not in a position to say, but that it was a great wrong and cannot bear the scrutiny of investigation I am satisfied. But that is the status of the government employee insofar as the right to strike is concerned.*

Cooperation on mutual problems is the way forward under voluntarism:

No man can carry on a great industry alone. No great fortune has been amassed through the efforts of one individual. The combined

* American Federationist, June 1915.
* Address, Mass Meeting, Washington, D.C., in behalf of salary increases for Government clerks, December 18, 1916.

minds of all associated together in the industry, their labor power, their cooperation and service are necessary to the success of the undertaking. Is there a man so impervious to the molding forces of the world in which he lives as to point to any one thing and say, "I, alone, did that?" Each of us is the heir of all the ages—none of us lives, acts, or thinks by himself alone. To ignore reality and to force upon the toilers a concept of individual isolation is to attempt to erect an opposition impervious to the meaning of natural forces and conditions that can only dam them back until the accumulated force sweeps aside everything.*

He expresses the value of what workers contribute to society thus:

Every day's work has been a demonstration that the workers can and do do things. They supply the creative power that is a necessary part of the process of material production. The work of their hands and brain is everywhere—buildings of industry and railroads that unite the distant parts of our country, the material agencies of transportation and communication, articles of daily food, use and wear, and in all of that which pertains to the material agencies of life and work. They have contributed something more than mechanical producing power. It is the mind and the insight controlling the muscles of the workers that give them value as producers and as members of society.*

The more successful union-management developments were based on prescribed principles and operated within the limits of constitutional provisions.

In addition to enabling workers to become free agents in the business world, American trade unions have frequently proposed such use of contract as would enable workers to participate with all other functional contributors in directing our market economy. This spirit reflected the absence in the U.S.A. of master-servant attitude and the sort of mutual confidence that can develop into union-management cooperation with understanding of mutual responsibilities. S. G. at no time advocated union control of industries. He was a confirmed believer in the need for hierarchy and a respecter of difference in functions. He was not misled by delusions about equality of men neither did he believe any man was fit to control the lives of his fellows.

* American Federationist, May 1914.
* American Federationist, February 1916.

9. Voluntarism

Decision to join a trade union constituted for the worker decision upon a way of life. Mr. Gompers contended the worker became a different individual who accepted responsibility for securing what he wanted for his work and social life and chose union membership as his method of securing things that had to be achieved jointly with other workers. The union itself and its operation became a joint responsibility of members and of their agents selected to carry on the work of the union as directed by the members.

In his own life and his teachings, service in the trade union movement was a primary way of expressing his ideals and human fellowship. Only by observing Christ's commandment to love one another can the trade unionist harmonize use of human freedom and of the collective action of the trade union in the best interests of society and of the long-time purposes of the union as an operating agency.

From basic belief in human freedom followed faith in voluntarism as the necessary method of procedure and action. Mr. Gompers seemed to assume man had a spirit that distinguished him from the other products which the Great Creator put into the world. The right and the exercise of freedom carried with them the duty of seeing a course through and the responsibility for at least trying to foresee and deal with its consequences.

He expressed his personal dedication to the cause thus:

In my early manhood a coterie of men, including myself, determined that under no circumstances should we be diverted from the purpose of devoting our efforts to the accomplishment of the best that could be secured in our time; that no allurement of office or emolument of business or speculation of any sort in which one solitary dollar was involved should lure us from devotion to human uplift and the best conception of American ideals.*

In an eight-hour pamphlet of 1905, he declares:

Permanent changes and progress must come from within man. You can't "save" people—they must save themselves. Unless the working people are organized to express their desires and needs and organized to express their will, any other method tends to weaken initiative.*

Voluntarism meant to him that decisions and policies of the union were the result of discussion and agreement and that the union relied upon educational methods for progress. This put a heavy responsibility on union officials for leadership in making the union a means of education, providing information and other data, speakers expert in various fields, and directing discussion along constructive lines. During the era of unrestricted immigration which paralleled the founding of the A. F. of L., unions served as a sort of Americanization agency, automatically teaching American customs and institutions so that new immigrants might become able to make informed decisions. Of course, no ideal is carried out rigidly or continuously by human agents.

In the early days, unions were organized, led and conducted by those who served without pay. The top officials carried their offices and their records in their pockets and the union more often than not met in a saloon or a room connected with one—the only free space available. If persons giving service were repaid for expenses they were fortunate. As the unions became more stable, their resources were larger and the need for unpaid services abated, but the need for voluntarism increased with the importance and the complexity of tasks and problems of the American Federation of Labor. Samuel Gompers gloried in declaring that neither he nor any executive of the American Federation of Labor had any authority over anybody nor the power to order anybody to do anything:

There is no power vested in the officers of the Federation. They

* Testimony, House Lobby Investigation Committee, Washington, D.C., December 1913.
* "The Workers and the Eight-Hour Workday," 1905.

can act in an advisory capacity; they can suggest; they can recommend. But they can not command one man in all America to do anything. Under no circumstances can they say, "You must do so and so," or, "You must desist from doing so and so." And this is true in the governmental affairs of the local organizations anywhere on the continent of America, industrially and politically.*

In the early days of the Federation resolution after resolution was introduced in annual conventions to compel hesitant or recalcitrant unions to comply with Federation decisions or rulings. Such resolutions were always the occasion for review and explanation of the policy of voluntarism, so that new delegates and new members had a chance for understanding. This debate and one on socialism became institutional events which members anticipated with eagerness—the older members who had learned to know and appreciate the principle gave testimony and the younger or newer ones noted arguments and accumulated facts for their own reports back home. Some of the abler leaders had developed oratory of a high order and all imitated Gompers who by mutual agreement closed all debates on fundamental principles. Gompers, who loved the English language, rarely indulged in slang but used the diction of a cultured Englishman and took pleasure in discriminating use of words.

Power of persuasion, accompanied by loyalty to the union and its purposes, and understanding of real self-interests, built up union discipline and made what Samuel Gompers once called a rope of sand the strongest trade union movement in the world. But that rope of sand had a leader who believed in men and loved them and who never wavered in his belief in their ability and competence for self-government. When jurisdictional disputes grew intense and threatened disruption of the Federation, when organized employers combined to destroy the Federation and there was betrayal from within, his faith in voluntarism grew stronger. He made it the heart of the message he prepared for what he knew would be his last American Federation of Labor convention and that convention recognized it as Gompers' Creed.

* American Federationist, December 1913. Abstract of testimony, House Lobby Investigation Committee.

He well knew that voluntarism depended upon disciplined responsibility in living and belief in the principles of self-government; it rested on understanding that persons who benefit through rights must respect the rights of others. Honesty and knowledge of moral law must continually develop to maintain voluntarism—the free life of human beings. An organization with a membership of two to three million persons convinced of the rightness of the cause and able to secure better conditions of life and work for their group strengthens the moral fibre of the nation.

GOMPERS' CREED

Forty-four years ago in the city of Pittsburgh a group of labor men met to bring to fruition an effort extending over a period of years—to organize a national labor movement. We were a group of labor men with little experience in a national labor movement. We had to find our problems and devise ways of meeting them. There was little to guide us. The majority of us had a standing in our local trade unions and in our national trade organizations, but we had not joined hands with the representatives of other trade organizations in an effort to make the labor movement a force in the determination of national policies.

The National Labor Union, like previous similar labor efforts, had organized a labor party and then passed out of existence. Industrialism growing out of constantly increasing invention of machinery, application of mechanical power which necessitated the factory system and the substitution of new materials for old, was making the need of economic protection for the workers increasingly imperative. Those of us who had opportunity to observe tendencies felt the responsibility to our fellow workers to make the effort for protection and for future progress.

There were but few paid trade union officials in those days, but after the day's work was done, those with the vision and spirit of service gave the evening hours and holidays to the cause of betterment of their fellow workers. More frequently than not the office of a trade union official was carried in his pocket and its code of laws in his heart and mind; benefits, even strike assistance, were irregular and undependable if provided at all; union dues and union rules varied from city to city, if not from shop to shop. The present trade union movement was then in the making—aye, had hardly begun.

But the men who constituted that Pittsburgh labor congress in 1881 were as brainy and resourceful a group as ever gathered; they were men who knew the joy and inspiration of service that entailed sacrifice. Service in the early trade union movement meant to become a marked man whom employers were reluctant to hire and who was discharged first; whose family must forego the comforts and often the necessaries of life; upon whose children the handicap attaching to the name of a "labor agitator" fell.

These very conditions of service in the labor movement assured the cause selected men of unusual qualities. They were men of self respect and character.

When the Pittsburgh labor congress set itself the task of planning an organization, it studied the British Trades Union Congress, drafted a similar plan and organized the Federation of Trades and Labor Unions of the United States and Canada. In our optimism we thought we had settled our economic problems and that we needed only to consider the field of labor legislation. We elected as our executive, a legislative committee, but provided no salaries, no permanent office, no full-time representatives. From year to year we met, accomplishing a little but keeping alive the thought of national organization and calling attention to the needs of the workers, until there came a crucial contest in which the existence of trade unions was threatened. Then the trade unions sent out the warning of danger and sent a small group to carry by word of mouth a message to rouse labor. Again in 1886 a national labor conference was called. This time it was designated a trade union conference to be composed of representatives of trade unions and to consider trade union problems. The deliberations of that conference resulted in the formation of our present American Federation of Labor with which the old Federation of Trades and Labor Unions was merged. This new federation recognized only the trade union card as a credential and proposed to deal primarily with economic problems. It was an organization that had no power and no authority except of a voluntary character. It was a voluntary coming together of unions with common needs and common aims. That feeling of mutuality has been a stronger bond of union than could be welded by any autocratic authority. Guided by voluntary principles our Federation has grown from a weakling into the strongest, best organized labor movement of all the world.

So long as we have held fast to voluntary principles and have been actuated and inspired by the spirit of service, we have sustained our forward progress and we have made our labor movement something to be respected and accorded a place in the councils of our Republic. Where we have blundered into trying to force a policy or a decision, even though wise and right, we have impeded, if not interrupted, the realization of our own aims.

But the very success of our organization has brought additional and serious dangers. Office in the labor movement now offers opportunity for something in addition to service—it offers opportunity for the self-seeker who sees an instrumentality for personal advancement both in the economic and in the political field. There are serious problems confronting us. Wisdom and conviction are necessary to wise decisions.

Men and women of our American trade union movement, I feel that I have earned the right to talk plainly with you. As the only delegate to that first Pittsburgh convention who has stayed with the problems of our movement through to the present hour, as one who with clean hands and with singleness of purpose has tried to serve the labor movement honorably and in a spirit of consecration to the cause of humanity, I want to urge devotion to the fundamentals of human liberty—the principles of voluntarism. No lasting gain has ever come from compulsion. If we seek to force, we but tear apart that which, united, is invincible. There is no way whereby our labor movement may be assured sustained progress in determining its policies and its plans other than sincere democratic deliberation until a unanimous decision is reached. This may seem a cumbrous, slow method to the impatient, but the impatient are more concerned for immediate triumph than for the education of constructive development.

Our movement has found these voluntary principles the secure foundation upon which the workers of all America make united effort, for our voluntary cooperation has ignored lines of political division separating the United States and Canada, because economically we are a unit. Because we refused to be bound by arbitrary restrictions or expedients we have fostered cohesive forces which give play to the finer and more constructive faculties of the peoples of both countries. We are eager to join in an international labor movement based upon the same principles of voluntarism. We are willing to cooperate if we can be assured a basis that will enable us to maintain our integrity—a condition necessary for our own virility and continued progress.

Understanding, patience, high-minded service, the compelling power of voluntarism have in America made what was but a rope of sand, a united, purposeful, integrated organization, potent for human welfare, material and spiritual. I have been with this movement since the beginning, for I have been given the privilege of service that has been accorded but few. Nor would that privilege have continued open to me had not service to the cause been my guiding purpose.

Events of recent months made me keenly aware that the time is not far distant when I must lay down my trust for others to carry forward. When one comes to close grips with the eternal things, there comes a new sense of relative values and the less worthy things lose significance. As I review the events of my sixty years of contact with the labor movement and as I survey the problems of today and study the opportunities of the future, I want to say to you, men and women of the American labor movement, do not reject the cornerstone upon which labor's structure has been builded—but base your all upon voluntary principles and illumine your every problem by consecrated devotion to that highest of all purposes— human well being in the fullest, widest, deepest sense.

We have tried and proved these principles in economic, political, social and international relations. They have been tried and not found wanting. Where we have tried other ways, we have failed.

A very striking illustration is emphasized by circumstances connected with the present location of our convention. For years force and selfish interests dominated relations across this international border, but the labor movement brought to an acute and difficult situation the spirit of patience and the desire of service and a transformation has been brought which gives us courage and conviction for wider application of the same principles. As we move upward to higher levels, a wider vision of service and responsibility will unfold itself. Let us keep the faith. There is no other way.*

* 1924 Convention Proceedings. Message written by Samuel Gompers and read by William Green.

10. No Compulsion

Strikes soon become a matter of public information and news through the press. Some employers and some users of products or services are inconvenienced. The strikers and their families more than other groups. In the case of public utilities or essential products widely used the strike is said to be affected by public interest and some form of compulsion or outside intervention is frequently proposed. Proposals containing some element of compulsion or creating some degree of government intervention and control were inevitably suggested for such strikes. Mr. Gompers' rejection of such proposals was equally inevitable. In his report to the 1900 Convention he explained his position:

It is submitted that the very terms, "arbitration" and "compulsory," stand in direct opposition to each other. Arbitration implies the voluntary action of two parties of diverse interests submitting to disinterested parties the question in dispute, or likely to come into dispute. Compulsion by any process, and particularly by the power of government, is repugnant to the principle as well as the policy of arbitration. If organized labor should fail to appreciate the danger involved in the proposed schemes of so-called compulsory arbitration, and consent to enactment of a law providing for its enforcement, there would be reintroduced the denial of the right of the workmen to strike in defense of their interests, and the enforcement by government of specific personal service and labor. In other words, under a law based upon compulsory arbitration, if an award were made against labor, no matter how unfair or unjust, and brought about by any means, no matter how questionable, we would be compelled to work or to suffer the state penalty, which might be either mulcting in damages, or going to jail; not one scintilla of distinction, not one jot removed from slavery.

It is strange how much men desire to compel other men to do by law. What we aim to achieve is freedom through organization. Arbitration is only possible when voluntary. It never can be successfully carried out unless the parties to a dispute or controversy are equals, or nearly equals, in power to protect and defend themselves, or to inflict injury upon the other.

The more thoroughly the workers are organized in their local and national unions, and federated by common bond, policy and polity, the better shall we be able to avert strikes and lockouts, secure conciliation, and if necessary, arbitration; but it must be voluntary arbitration, or there should be no arbitration at all.

It is our aim to avoid strikes; but I trust that the day will never come when the workers of our country will have so far lost their manhood and independence as to refuse to strike, regardless of the provocation, or to surrender their right to strike. We seek to prevent strikes, but we realize that the best means by which they can be averted is to be the better prepared for them. We endeavor to prevent strikes; but there are some conditions far worse than strikes, and among them is a demoralized, degraded and debased manhood.*

Mr. Gompers also opposed as unequally handicapping workers, legislation which required delay in strikes until a disinterested or public inquiry could be made together with recommendations. An investigation is only a means of securing publicity and in itself has little effect upon securing industrial justice, said Mr. Gompers, and summarized his opposition thus:

Laws must not invade personal rights and liberty. The ownership of a free man is vested in himself alone. The free man's ownership of himself involves his labor power. In fact the only difference between a free man and a slave is the right to sell or withhold his labor power. This precious right must be cherished and guarded against all invasions. It is of greater value than all other purposes or ends. When any workmen or number of workmen are compelled by law to work one month, one week, one day, or one hour against their own volition, then there has ensued and been established slavery.*

Compulsory investigation legislation is identical in principle with compulsory arbitration; the difference is only one of degree. Compulsory arbitration makes strikes illegal and strikers criminal for all time instead of for a definite period . . . Under either, men who refuse to work for any reason, who refuse to perform involuntary servitude may be fined and imprisoned. . . . Stripped of all sophistry and all verbiage, compulsory investigation or compulsory arbitration resolve themselves into compulsory service.*

* From President's report, Convention Proceedings, 1900.
* American Federationist, February 1913.
* American Federationist, October 1916.

To those who advocate restrictions on strikes in the public interest by means of disinterested or public fact finding and decision:

After all, is the public disinterested? Do we not rather find it composed of different groups, some whose interests are similar to those of the employers involved, and who hence naturally sympathize with them and their position? There are many whose financial welfare is identical with that of the employer, who are dependent upon his prosperity. There are many whose industrial experience as workmen would inevitably predispose them to approve the actions and demands of the employees upon any question. There are many selfish and indifferent to the moral and ethical values of any issue that conflicts with their own comfort. There are some few with broader sympathies and keener and deeper understanding of human nature, who try to maintain the dispassionate attitude of justice toward both, but upon some critical and vital issue can they completely overcome the formative, determining influences of environment, instruction, and the indefinable psychic influences of their own kind? It is a serious and dangerous matter to entrust the determination of issues which concern the life, the happiness, the welfare, and freedom of the workers into the hands of other men who do not and can not know the toiler's world in which they live, move and have their being!*

Especially significant in this period of controlled public opinion is his editorial observation of 1913:

To public opinion is often attributed a sort of sanctity, a divine origin, an attribute that formerly was attributed to conscience. We have learned that the individual's conscience depends upon his environment, his inherited qualities, his education, and is not something absolute, divine, or different in nature from other faculties. So we also know that *vox populi* is not necessarily *vox dei,* but may be made to approach it as freedom of expression, openness of mind, and truths are allowed to prevail. Public opinion is not a unity but there are various opinions held by different groups making up the public. That group which presents its convictions most persuasively or most insistently, controls the prevailing policy. Conceptions of truths vary with the opportunities and the understanding of the individual or the group. As a group that is a part of the public becomes more influential, able to express more forcibly and clearly its ideals and concepts of justice and truths—things the group has evolved from its

* American Federationist, January 1913.

labor and daily life with other men—that group may alter the trend and scope of public opinion until it reflects more completely the life and welfare of all mankind. Frequently public opinion is only a prevailing sentiment, determined by convenience or ignorance. Sometimes it is only a "snap" judgment based on incorrect data.*

Disinterestedness or remoteness from the effect of solutions does not assure wisdom or equity. Those directly concerned and with the intimate information born of operations—workers and management—were in the best position to give justice. He believed the unions' problem was to get these two forces to operate promptly and effectively.

Mr. Gompers did not content himself with opposition to compulsory arbitration, but he associated himself with a group of persons of similar convictions and who banded together to make voluntary conciliation and arbitration freely accessible: The National Civic Federation. This was a private association which performed some of the services a governmental department of labor usually provides. This organization had no formal membership or dues, and was merely a channel through which persons believing in personal freedom and its goal cooperated. The Socialists bitterly attacked it because they could not conceive of mutual interests of wage-earners and employers any more than they could understand voluntarism. It was an organization which provided Samuel Gompers with a public platform on which he could freely speak his mind to employers on matters affecting labor's interests. It provided the Federation with facilities to implement voluntary arbitration. Its last important service to him was to facilitate employers' cooperation in the work of his war labor committees which assisted him as a member of the Advisory Committee to the Council for National Defense.

Meanwhile under his leadership the American Federation of Labor was diligently promoting legislation to authorize a federal Department of Labor to be headed by a Secretary—a member of the President's Cabinet. This law was enacted in 1913 and initially gave organized labor representation in the Executive Branch of the United States Government.

* American Federationist, February 1913.

11. Strikes

As Samuel Gompers often said, the fundamental difference between a free worker and a slave is the right to strike, and also warned:

Strikes ought to be, and in well organized trade unions they are, the last means which working men resort to to protect themselves.*

He repeatedly declared that:

The most potent factor to prevent or reduce the number of strikes is a well organized trade union with a full treasury ready to strike should the necessity arise.*

In addition he pointed to the value of right-timing:

To know when to strike and particularly when not to strike, is a science not yet fully understood.*

Nevertheless with all the losses and hardships strikes involved to wage-earners, employers and the public, he raised the real issue in the alternative:

Is it the part of wisdom, is it the course of right for any period of time to compel the workman to give involuntary servitude so that the companies may operate their railroad and perform their obligation to society?*

Strikes as he knew meant losses, inconvenience, frequently suffering to all concerned. Therefore unions developed conventions and machinery that assured deliberation and informed action in calling strikes. When the die was cast he had little sympathy with weaklings. The "scab"

* Senate Committee on Relations between Labor and Capital, August 18, 1883.
* President's report, Convention Proceedings 1888.
* 1888 Convention Proceedings.
* Testimony, Senate Interstate Commerce Commission. Threatened railway strike, August 31, 1916.

or the person who did not conform to union policy he denounced in scathing terms:

> And let me say this, that I hold that a man who is a traitor to his country is upon a par with the scab to his trade.*

He opposed proposals to limit or deny the right to strike because he believed freedom was not divisible. He said editorially:

> What the right of resistance to injustice is in the political world, the right to strike, to cease work, is in the industrial.*

Because he believed freedom was the basic attribute of a human being he opposed without reservation any compulsory regulation restriction or denial of the right to strike for any period. To safeguard this right Gompers advised workers in times of national emergencies to forego voluntarily the use of their right, as in World War I his leadership and counsel resulted in the equivalent of a no-strike pledge to the President of the United States.

Mr. Gompers advised provisions in trade union agreements for voluntary arbitration to supplement collective bargaining between employers and workers. He did not oppose investigation with publicity for recommendations by disinterested parties when collective bargaining broke down.

> A strike is for the purpose of gaining some definite, concrete improvement in working conditions. The strike movement succeeds or fails in proportion to its effectiveness in accomplishing the purpose for which it was inaugurated. If a strike results in tangible benefits, those benefits are definitely formulated in the agreement by which the contest ends and industrial peace is restored.

> These industrial contracts between workers and employers are the mile-stones of industrial progress. They clinch each forward movement in a tangible form and become a new basis for future demands and movements for greater progress.

> An economic movement to be successful must be under the control of directors who understand the technique of the labor movement and who know the effectiveness of every move. It is a very dangerous thing in time of strike to advise workers to "raise hell." If that leader does not know what to do with the "hell" after

---

* Speech, 1917, accepting the presidency of American Alliance for Labor and Democracy, Minneapolis, Minn.

* American Federationist, January 1913.

strikers have raised it, he has embroiled those workers in a very dangerous condition—a condition that may endanger the whole movement.

Efforts to put "the fear of God" into the hearts of those who have no regard for human rights may have a place in the movement for human progress, but how, what, and by whom? There's the rub.

The hope of the workers lies in definite, persistent, intelligent and constructive action along lines that lead to definite, beneficial results to the workers—to the masses of the people—hence, to the glory and perpetuation of our great Republic.*

A strike he interpreted in calm rational terms thus:

Let a man have the right to decide when he is to work or is not to work, and let that decision be backed by his power to keep himself from being obliged by immediate necessity to offer his labor to an employer, and the consequence must be that he will not sell his labor-power until the terms offered him are the best that the industry can warrant.*

With regard to strikes in war-time he submitted this guide:

Our country is now facing a crisis to meet which continuity of production is essential. Workers, decide every industrial question fully mindful of those men—fellow Americans—who are on the battle line, facing the enemies' guns, needing munitions of war to fight the battle for those of us back home, doing work necessary but less hazardous. No strike ought to be inaugurated that can not be justified to the men facing momentary death. A strike during the war is not justified unless principles are involved equally fundamental as those for which fellow citizens have offered their lives— their all.*

PICKETING

Picketing—or the right of free speech—was an important adjunct of the strike in Gompers' thinking. It enabled strikers to warn potential strike-breakers as well as customers who might not know what was involved in the contest.

Courts finally accepted peaceful picketing as legal and defined "peaceful."

* American Federationist, November 1916.
* President's report, Convention Proceedings, 1910.
* American Federationist, May 1918.

What is picketing? It is the stationing of certain members of trade unions near factories or establishments involved in strikes (or lockouts) for the purpose of inducing, persuading and prevailing upon non-union men to respect the cause of labor and refrain from taking the places vacated by the unionists. How can this be lawful? It is certainly the right of strikers or their sympathizers to use the public highway peaceably and in a way not obstructive of the equal rights of others . . .

Union labor asserts the legal and moral. . . . right to strike and to boycott. None of these weapons is necessarily offensive, but they are all clearly defenses. Violence is not a recognized part of labor's plan of campaign. There can be no success for any strike or boycott which defends an assault on person and property. Labor needs to be strong through numbers, effective organization, the justice of its cause, and the reasonableness of its methods. It relies on moral suasion, because of its conviction that its demands are generally equitable, and picketing is as necessary to the employment of moral influence as the boycott is necessary to the proper use of the moral power wielded by labor and its sympathizers.*

The right to picket is essential to secure an understanding or even a hearing for many an industrial dispute. Cooperation and unity of action among workers must be based upon knowledge of facts and purposes . . .

To deny the wage-earners the right to tell their story by word of mouth in the streets, public highways or public places is to deny them a right necessary to carry out the purposes of the labor movement.*

BOYCOTT

In addition to strikes and picketing trade unions exert economic power by advising for the purchase of products made under union conditions and against purchase of products made under unfair conditions. The union may advise its members and other purchasers against buying specific products and it may advise other unions that a company making specific products they handle is unfair. S. G. gave the following recommendations to those promoting such boycotts:

Every local organization seems to take upon itself the right to levy boycotts and spread them before the entire country. It seems

* Testimony, House Judiciary Committee, March 26, 1900.
* Article for use Washington State bill on picketing, January 11, 1916.

to me that before people should be asked to taboo a product of any firm, opportunity should be given for investigation, and no boycott recognized unless approved by the Conventions, or the Executive Council in the interim of the Conventions of the Federation.

The boycott is a very powerful weapon in the hands of the wage workers, but if put on a firm unfairly, promiscuously or without investigation it is likely to react upon us and destroy the usefulness of that method to obtain our rights.*

Boycotts were effective and employers frequently sought protection of the law against the consequences instead of dealing with causes through collective bargaining. Lawyers soon found boycotting a fertile and complicated field of legal precedents. S. G. told the Federal Commission on Industrial Relations:

Workmen have a right to say that they will not patronize those who are unfriendly to them and those who support their adversaries. This is all that boycotting implies. There is no aggression here, no criminal purpose, and no criminal way of accomplishing a proper purpose.*

He further explained legal implications:

Had the union threatened to do anything it had no right to do; had it maliciously libeled the defendant and injured him by such libel, a different case would have been presented. But men may "conspire" to do any act which is itself lawful. They may "conspire" to tell the truth. They may "threaten" to exercise their rights. The result may be an injury to the person threatened or denounced or complained of, but such injury is the result of his own conduct, or the incidental effect of ordinary competition, and the law does not undertake to prevent such injuries or punish those who inflict them. If it did, it would destroy individual and industrial liberty.*

He urged safeguards for the rights of others:

It is well to bear in mind that this weapon of labor (the boycott) is most potent, and one which should be exercised with the greatest degree of care, and with an intense purpose to be absolutely just. An unjust or inconsiderate boycott does more to injure the cause of labor than a hundred victories achieved through its agency. Whenever an application has been submitted to head-

* President's report, 1891 Convention Proceedings.
* Testimony, Industrial Commission, Washington, D.C., April 18, 1899.
* American Federationist, March 1901.

quarters an investigation was instituted and the concern complained against given an opportunity to state its version of the matters in dispute. In no case has a concern been placed upon our "We Don't Patronize" list until it has had an opportunity to be heard in its own defense. In each of the letters to employers upon these subjects it was accompanied by the suggestion of an adjustment mutually honorable and advantageous, and tendering, if necessary, our good offices to accomplish that purpose.*

Men have a right to do business, but this is one-half of the truth. The men with whom business is done have the right to withdraw and transfer their custom. This is the other half, which is always ignored in anti-boycott arguments. Keep the two halves in view and boycotting on any scale and for any reason becomes a direct, unavoidable deduction.

Labor claims the right to suspend dealings with any and all who refuse to support what it considers its legitimate demand. The decisions are confused, and the question is new, but ultimately the right of any man to do with his patronage what he pleases must be recognized.*

The organized wage-worker moves by two cardinal moral principles. The first is: His right, if he is a free man, to dispose of his labor power as he wills. The second is: His right, if he is not a slave, to dispose of his purchasing power as he chooses. And what is the right of one man is the right of many.*

VIOLENCE

He repeatedly issued grave warning against violence:

We denounce and oppose violence. If any individual in a union commits a crime we expect the officers of the law to enforce the law. Any attempt on our part to apply discipline would be prejudicing his case before it went to the jury. The labor union deals with the economic conditions of work; the Government, representing the whole of society, deals with questions of law and order. Organized labor asks for no exemptions from the law, but it protests against distortions of the law by the courts.*

He also held:

I am fully convinced that there is nothing so hurtful to the

* President's report, Convention Proceedings, 1897.
* Testimony, Industrial Commission, Washington, D.C., April 18, 1899.
* American Federationist, November 1910.
* Interview, James Creelman, New York World, June 7, 1903.

interests of organized working men as the use of physical force in their efforts to secure justice—attacks upon life or property. The men who are active in the labor movement in this country realize that fact and urge it on every conceivable occasion. As a matter of fact it is seldom that a union man on strike makes an attack upon a non-union man.*

As to whether strikes should be prohibited workers employed on undertakings affected by public interest, S. G. said:

The difference between a strike where the public is not inconvenienced and where it is should have no bearing on the justice of the dispute . . . Should the public deny justice to those who may have to strike?*

The American labor movement has made a clear differentiation between government workers and private employment, holding that in private employment the strike is the last resort, while in government employment, legislation is the final remedy.*

SYMPATHETIC STRIKE

He met and defined policy with respect to the sympathetic strike in 1894. A dual union of railway workers went on strike against the Pullman Company. The Pullman Company from the privileged position of a monopoly had refused to deal with regular railway unions and had refused a fair share of earnings to their employees. The strike leader sought aid in the form of a national sympathetic strike. S. G. knew a sympathetic strike would invalidate contracts with a serious backset to union-management negotiations. He called a meeting of his Executive Council for Chicago—strike headquarters. In spite of their resentment of Federal troops, Federal injunction and the strong fraternal ties between unions, the Executive Council believed the proposed sympathetic strike would practically destroy their constructive labor movement. The Council issued a statement containing this declaration:

The trade union movement is one of reason, one of deliberation, and depending entirely upon the voluntary and sovereign action of its members . . .

* Interview, James Creelman, New York World, June 7, 1903.
* From "New York World," November 22, 1919.
* American Federationist, January 1918.

Industrial contests cannot be entered into at the behest of any individual officer of this conference, regardless of the position he may occupy in our organizations. Strikes in our affiliated organizations are entered into only as a last resort and after all peaceful adjustment of grievances have failed, and then only after the members have by their own votes (usually requiring a two-thirds and often a three-fourths vote) so decided . . .

While we may not have the power to order a strike of the working people of our country, we are fully aware that a recommendation from this conference to them to lay down their tools of labor would largely influence the members of our affiliated organizations; and appreciating the responsibility resting upon us and the duty we owe to all, we declare it to be the sense of this conference that a general strike at this time is inexpedient, unwise and contrary to the best interests of the working people. We further recommend that all connected with the American Federation of Labor now out on sympathetic strike should return to work, and those who contemplate going out on sympathetic strike are advised to remain at their usual vocations.*

Mr. Gompers and the Executive Council also condemned the United States for using its powers—troops and federal injunction—to defeat the strikers and to aid the corporation.

To the criticism that his position was lacking in idealism, Mr. Gompers replied:

To make contracts and stick to them even when they limit or take away the right of striking out of sympathy is not to sacrifice idealism. To consult actual conditions and the dictates of reasonable experience before striking or making demands on employers is not to abandon any ideal ever proposed by an intelligent trade unionist.*

It is important to note that in the Pullman situation unions were advised to fulfill their contractual obligations while in the case of action in support of the right of Negro longshoremen to negotiate with their employers the sympathetic strike was approved—because of the importance attached to protection against racial discrimination and the local strength of trade unions made success possible.

* Extracts from statement issued by a conference of the A. F. of L. Executive Council and Presidents of international unions, July 13, 1894.
* American Federationist, October 1904, page 154.

POLITICAL STRIKE

S. G. made a declaration on political or general strikes before the British Trades Union Congress in Britain in 1919: (He termed the political strike "direct action.")

The American trade union movement . . . are profoundly convinced that the policy of direct action cannot lead to permanent success . . .

In a country where the political life is democratic, as it is in England and in the United States, the undermining of the democratic political structure by direct action methods is not only unwise but impracticable and destructive. Our own direct actionists in America express their philosophy in the slogan, "Strike at the ballot-box with an axe." There seems little difference between this idea and that expressed by British advocates of direct action. They interpreted direct action to mean the use of the strike to secure political demands which could not or had not been secured through political channels.

The political system both in England and in the United States offers a periodical and absolutely free opportunity for arriving at decisions on political questions. It offers a method by which majority decision may be registered for or against any proposition within the realm of politics and any proposition whether wise or unwise can be carried into effect providing the majority can be convinced of its desirability.

The philosophy of direct action contemplates nothing short of substitution of minority rule for majority rule. It seems incredible that in either England or America there should be seriously contemplated any system by which the minority could through forcible measures, invalidate and overturn the expressed will of the majority. What is meant by direct action is this:

In the event that the majority decision at the ballot-box goes against any given proposition, the minority may, by suspending work in a vital industry, compel the nation to reverse the decision of the majority and accede to the will of the minority . . .

It is the conviction of the American people and specifically of the American working people that political democracy as we know it is the best form of government yet devised and that it must not be endangered and cannot be endangered without entailing the most serious consequences to everyone . . .

The destruction of the democratic political structure by direct action would inevitably lead to chaos out of which we could not emerge into the restoration of order without first restoring the political structure that had been destroyed.

History records but few ideas more tragic and more fantastic than the idea of government by direct action. It is in fundamental opposition to everything that we have learned through experience to cherish and safeguard. The strike itself is a weapon too valuable and too sacred to be used for any other than its legitimate purpose. It is a weapon which the workers of the world will never relinquish, however much they may hope to decrease the necessity for its use.

And the working people, of the United States, at least, will reserve the strike as a weapon to be used with wisdom and for constructive purposes. Destroying political democracy can not, by any interpretation, be called constructive or productive of permanent benefit, and of this truth the American trade union movement is profoundly convinced.*

Mr. Gompers was just as emphatic in condemning direct or economic action to attain a political objective as he was in opposing a sympathetic strike in the Pullman situation in 1894. His purpose, he said, was "to safeguard political democracy, the best form of government yet devised." But what would he have counseled had that "form" become only an outward symbol for a "highly controlled democracy" as acute observers abroad say? What would he have counselled if or when that "form" became only an outer shell concealing a purpose to modify justice and abolish rights which our constitution was designed to provide? What would he have counselled if powerful organized groups threatened the existence of our western civilization, its code of civilized behavior, personal freedom, religion and even the right to possess one's mind and conscience? Would the forms of democracy be more sacred than individual freedom and potentiality or would Gompers have urged and led "a remnant of the population to save us from reaction and barbarism"? Few principles are absolutes— even majority rule which can be a tyranny over minorities or may be manipulated by controlling sources of information. It is the inner spirit or substance that matters. Gompers always recognized that a few often did so much and that the majority need not be infallibly correct.

* Statement before British Trades Union Congress, September 10, 1919; reported, American Federationist, October 1919, pp. 962–964.

12. Road Block to Contractual Relations—Jurisdictional Disputes

JURISDICTIONAL DISPUTES

Jurisdictional disputes put faith in voluntarism to crucial tests. They usually arise out of technical changes and are not due just to perversities of human nature. S. G. emphatically declared:

The invention of a new machine or a new tool, or the discovery of some substitute article, frequently changes and transforms the labor of one craft, or form of labor, to another, and it is easily understood that men and organizations look with jealous care not only for the maintenance of their organizations, but that they also encounter considerable difficulty in conforming themselves and their organizations to the new conditions. It has been my constant aim to endeavor to aid our fellow-unionists in finding a way out of the difficulties by which they are confronted, or to bring about an agreement, even though it be temporary, in the hope that time would aid in solving the problems.*

Describing the services of the Executive Council in helping to settle trade union disputes, S. G. said:

We believed that we were the servants of the working people, obliged to do their bidding, and not to arrogate to ourselves the functions of dictators, directing our fellow working people.*

S. G. early began to consider industrial federation of trade unions as a way to facilitate adjustment to jurisdictional disputes. In 1888 he made this suggestion:

The thought has frequently occurred to me whether in the near future the basis of our Federation should not be modeled upon a somewhat different basis from the present one, by having the various industries classified by the divisions of these industries: such as, for instance, the iron, steel or metal industry to have a convention of the representatives of all the trade unions in that industry; the building trades to have their convention . . . the

* President's Report, 1901 Convention proceedings.
* President's Report, 1888 Convention proceedings.

railroad employees theirs, and so on, each legislating upon the questions that affect the general interests of their particular trades and interests; these industrial divisions to be in turn represented by their proportionate number of delegates in the convention of the American Federation of Labor, and a representative of each industry elected a member of the Executive Council. The conventions of the industrial divisions might be held simultaneously in different halls, of course, but in the city in which the Federation would hold its convention immediately after their adjournment. The idea may not be practical for immediate adoption, but discussion of it can only lead to good results. One thing is certain—the autonomy of each trade and industrial division would thus be more firmly secured.*

This proposal for industrial departments was never adopted as a whole. As unions felt the need of departments to deal with common problems and adjust jurisdictional issues they formulated constitutions containing some of the constructive provisions of Gompers' proposal. Still laboring with this problem a bit later he advised the convention:

The last convention declared that organizations having disputes of this character should meet by representatives, and endeavor to arrive at an adjustment before cognizance could be taken of the matter by the American Federation of Labor. While quite a number have acquiesced in this suggestion, yet I have found that in many instances the organization which has benefited by any change and has possessed the power has manifested an unwillingness to meet with the organization whose trade has been the loser. Then again, there is a tendency among too many of our affiliated unions to extend their jurisdiction over branches of trade already organized under another head.*

Of course it is evident that in some instances there are two or more organizations which should and could, with advantage, be consolidated or amalgamated into one, and efforts by such organizations should certainly be made, assisted or initiated by the American Federation of Labor, but I submit that it is untenable and intolerable for an organization to attempt to ride rough shod over and trample under foot the rights and jurisdiction of a trade the jurisdiction of which is already covered by an existing organization . . .

The interests of the wage earners of the craft, to promote and protect which the organizations were primarily formed, have no

* President's report, 1888 Convention Proceedings.
* President's report, 1901 Convention Proceedings.

moral right, from a trade union point of view, to be jeopardized by pursuing a policy in an attempt at trade invasion made without the knowledge or consent of the crafts involved.*

The employers' interests should not be imperilled:

It is trade union law and policy that fair employers desirous of living upon terms of amity with organized labor should not be made to suffer from inter-trade union disputes.*

He protested industrial organization as an addition to craft unions which perform distinctive and needed functions:

Industrial unionism is not a cure for disputes or differences between organizations of workers. That form of organization would only transfer disputed questions to other boundaries and other terms. Jurisdictional disputes develop from necessary changes in organization and differences of opinions as to the best way of meeting the difficulty. They are an inevitable accompaniment of growth and organization. The problem is not to eliminate jurisdictional disputes, for that would eliminate life, but to meet them in the best possible way.

The element essential to the adjustment of these disputes is the spirit of fraternity among workers, mindful of common interests and desirous of reaching adjustments. The workers must be willing to go along together and work out practical agreements. This spirit was one of the distinguishing characteristics of the San Francisco convention. Although there were proposals to use compulsion, to revoke charters, to dictate terms of adjustment, yet the true spirit of voluntary organization prevailed and the workers agreed to remain within the American labor movement and to work out their differences with regard for common interests and for the maintenance of the power and effectiveness of the organization.*

When a proposal was made to suspend the Carpenters' Brotherhood in connection with a jurisdictional dispute, S. G. warned:

I have looked askance for a considerable period of time at the constant extension of claims of jurisdiction on the part of the Brotherhood of Carpenters and Joiners. Many of their claims to jurisdiction are unwarranted. But they are not the only offenders . . .

This is the second recommendation of the committee within

* President's report, 1902 Convention Proceedings.
* President's report, 1905 Convention Proceedings.
* American Federationist, January 1916.

the past few hours for the revocation of charters of international unions. Where are you going to stop? . . .

Is it not significant to every delegate in this convention that the Committee on Adjustment has reported to this convention that the Brotherhood of Carpenters and Joiners should be suspended from the American Federation of Labor? . . . Is that not something to make us pause to see whither we are drifting?

Is it not possible that, with full affiliation with this American Federation of Labor, with our ties and bonds of unionism, with our personal ties and strong friendships, we might be able to have some influence upon the Carpenters, and upon other organizations, in order that they may limit themselves in their unwarrantable extension of jurisdiction?

I had in mind striking out the words: "The Brotherhood of Carpenters and Joiners shall stand suspended until such time as this decision is complied with," and substitute the words: "If they fail to carry out the instructions of this convention the displeasure and the censure of the American Federation of Labor will be expressed for the unwarrantable attitude assumed by the Brotherhood of Carpenters and Joiners" . . .

I have expressed to you what I believe should be the insistent demand of the trade unionists represented in this convention, and the trade unionists of the country and of the continent, who are looking to this convention to maintain the integrity of our movement and not to take any action that shall make for its dismemberment.

Men and women, we need have no fear of the enemies of organized labor from the outside. We can stand their antagonism, their vilification, their opposition, their attempts to destroy us— the danger is not from without. Like every mass movement in the history of the world, every people's movement, every workers' movement, the danger of its disintegration is from within. Let us not fail to appreciate the lessons of history. Bear in mind that though our American Federation of Labor is the best, most intelligent, most practical movement of the workers of this or any other country, of this or any other time, we are not safe from disintegration and failure if we do not appreciate the value of human weakness, of human strength, of human will, of human selfishness, of human greed, of human altruism, as well as the high ideals of human brotherhood. Don't let us make a mistake, don't let us put up a rock upon which this great ship of labor shall be wrecked.

There are hearts and souls yearning for the greater strength of our movement and its further development—the unorganized even that are not with us now . . .

Men of labor, don't destroy their hopes for the future.*

In 1902 there were so many and such menacing disputes S. G. made this report to the convention:

Beyond doubt the greatest problem, the danger, which above all others most threatens not only the success, but the very existence of the American Federation of Labor, is the question of jurisdiction. I may truly record the fact that never for one moment since the formation of our Federation have I entertained a doubt or misgiving as to the growth, success and permanency of the American Federation of Labor, and I would not now be apprehensive of its future were it not forced upon my deliberate judgment, which has developed into a firm conviction, that unless our affiliated National and International Unions radically and soon change their course we shall at no distant day be in the midst of an internecine contest unparalleled in any era of the industrial world, aye, not even when workmen of different trades were arrayed against each other behind barricades in the streets over the question of trade against trade. They mutually regarded each (other) with hatred and treated each other as mortal enemies . . .

No combination of labor's enemies need cause us the apprehension which this fratricidal strife does in the claims made by unions for the extension of their trade jurisdiction.

There is scarcely an affiliated organization which is not engaged in a dispute with another organization (and in some cases with several organizations) upon the question of jurisdiction. It is not an uncommon occurrence for an organization, and several have done so quite recently, to so change their laws and claims to jurisdiction as to cover trades never contemplated by the organization's officers or members; never comprehended by their title; trades of which there is already in existence a national union. And this without a word of advice, counsel or warning . . .

This contention for jurisdiction has grown into such proportions and is fought with such intensity as to arouse the most bitter feuds and trade wars. In many instances employers fairly inclined toward organized labor have been made innocently to suffer from causes entirely beyond their control, and other employers again, have taken advantage of the first inception of the fancy or notion for "expansion" of trade jurisdiction, fanned it into a flame and taking advantage of the excitement and hatred of the war against each other, refused to recognize either organization, pretending to claim it a war among labor organizations with which they do not

* 1915 Convention Proceedings, pp. 408–410.

wish to interfere. On the surface the employer's claim appears tenable, but in their hearts they enjoy the situation by which their pockets are enriched. Nevertheless the employers' contention in regard to this question cannot be disputed.*

IMPORTANCE OF TRADE AUTONOMY

The principle which Samuel Gompers preserved throughout this troubled period was trade autonomy—or the right of a national trade union to control of its own rules and funds. Self government in special fields or for special functions requires due regard for an identical right of similar groups. Such self restraint is the key to the permanence in freemen's institutions:

We assert that it is the duty, as it is also the plain interest, of all working people to organize as such, meet in council, and to take practical steps to effect the unity of the working class, as an indispensable preliminary to any successful attempt to eliminate the evils of which we, as a class, so bitterly and justly complain. That this much-desired unity has never been achieved is owing in a great measure to the non-recognition of the autonomy, or the right of self-government, of the several trades. The American Federation of Labor, however, avoids the fatal rock on which previous organizations, having similar aims, have split, by simply keeping in view this fundamental principle as a landmark, which none but the most infatuated would have ever lost sight of.*

His policies show he realized solution of any jurisdictional question had to proceed with consideration for the structural security of the organization in order to provide the cement of consent of those concerned.

* President's Report, Convention Proceedings, 1902.
* A. F. of L. circular "Labor Omnia Vincit," 1894.

13. No Discrimination

Mr. Gompers had a very deep appreciation of the injustices heaped upon underprivileged and minority groups. Where discrimination was due to race, sex and religion he could be relied on to support a movement for justice. He helped Hebrew workers to organize and recognized that exclusively Jewish unions would help their groups to grow into the trade union movement. Likewise with Negroes although he steadily reminded such arrangement should be temporary only. As to women wage earners though he believed the home was a pillar of society, conditions often made it necessary for women to become bread winners also. While he "went along with" protective laws for women wage earners, he believed such women would be better protected by joining trade unions and assuming with male workers the responsibilities of securing justice and promoting their work interest. He urged trade unions to open membership to all workers employed in their jurisdictions. Unions like all other institutions were often slow in making equal opportunity available. But he recognized that all rules must have occasional exceptions. He waived two union principles preventive of discrimination in order to help an underprivileged group gain equal opportunity to organize when he sponsored a Federation charter for the United Hebrew Trades—a dual central body with exclusively racial basis for membership.

When the United Hebrew Trades rejected a trade union ruling of the American Federation of Labor, Gompers went before them, declared their charter revoked and stated the A.F. of L. policy thus:

Now, let me say this to you, that in the United States of America there must not be the judgment of a Jewish labor movement, no more than there must be the judgment of the Catholic labor movement, no more than there must be the judgment of a

Protestant labor movement, no more than there must be a judgment of a Buddhist or an atheist labor movement. The labor movement of America must prevail . . .

To me it matters not whether a man be a Protestant or a Catholic, or a free thinker, or an atheist. That is a matter of his own conscience and of his own judgment, his own hopes or his own fears, but I do say that in the labor movement we are not Jews nor Christians nor atheists but we are working men and bound by the common ties.*

He also acted for withdrawal of this special privilege later and advised the Jewish unions against dual allegiance:

It is the duty of the Jewish workers of America to become citizens of this land, to adopt its customs and ways and with whatever effectiveness is within their power to help in the development and progress of higher ideals and institutions for this land which has helped them so much in the struggle for better things. Let the members of the United Hebrew Trades adopt this as their fatherland and give it the same fervent devoted loyalty that they have ever given to all that they have held dear. Let them turn their backs upon the Old Zion and the old conceptions and turn their faces toward liberty and freedom, industrial and political, and in their united might fight for the realization of this new purpose, a new Zion that shall mean for them and all Jewish workers better lives in this world and better lives for their children and their children's children.

Put into the daily task and into the relations of fellow workers the same glorifying spirit of poetry and exaltation that has given Jewish music and literature its rare inspiration and power, and by so doing make the United Hebrew Trades Organization a power that shall sweep all injustice from the lives of all Hebrew workers, however humble, native born or strangers in our gateway city. Hebrews have been ever mighty men and women in the world's history, may you be like the great of the race.*

This policy of excluding discussion of religious faith from union business carried with it obligation to maintain in the union—the agency of common action—the moral code of western culture and civilization. The union became identical with religion to many workers.

*American Federationist, June 1915, p. 424.
* Address, United Hebrew Trades, May 10, 1915. New York. American Federationist, June 1915, p. 424.

The right of an individual to the religion of his own choice was scrupulously observed in Federation union rule and practice. However, he guarded against becoming anti-religious. Under his leadership every session of Federation Conventions was opened by prayer. Representatives of prevailing faiths were invited to serve in rotation without prejudice. Non-discrimination did not become secularization.

Discrimination on the basis of race, creed, sex, political party or nationality would have complicated effective action on wages and hours. Such discrimination was impossible for unions which had to organize the stream of workers flowing through our immigration ports from nearly every part of the world. In 1912, S. G. reported to the Rochester Convention:

Some months ago the American Federation of Labor inaugurated a campaign of education among the steel workers of the United States and Canada, with the purpose of bringing this great number of toilers into the beneficent and protective fold of the trade union movement. The history of the antagonism of the great steel companies toward the organization of their employees is a matter of common knowledge. Their evident purpose being to thwart any attempt made to organize the workers or for them to organize themselves, the plan of employing workmen speaking foreign tongues was adopted. The steel corporations, by the intermingling of the various races, nearly all endowed with pronounced racial characteristics, consider that these differences in temperament will provide an effectual barrier to successful organization. These workmen, many of whom are untutored, born in lands of oppression, surrounded by squalor, inured to hardship, reaching manhood without that full mental development which makes for independence and self-preservation, are lured to America. Upon arrival in this English-speaking country, the light of our civilization but slowly dawns upon them. The rights to which the American citizen is entitled are unknown to them—the struggle for subsistence being the great necessity. With languages not easily understood, and various tongues spoken in a single steel plant, it is not to be wondered that the workers' comprehension of the rights to which they are entitled comes as an exceedingly slow process.*

Powerful industries made agreements with shipping

* President's Report, Convention Proceedings, 1912.

companies to bring over annually new supplies of workers, varying the countries periodically so as to preserve language as a barrier to inter-group communication. These new immigrants crowded the ranks of "unskilled" workers and necessitated foreign-speaking organizers and foreign language literature.

Samuel Gompers was frankly a partisan of Negroes. Arriving in New York City in the midst of race riots resulting from conscription for the Civil War, he saw his father nearly mobbed for shaking hands with a Negro who had done him a kindly service. In New York he lived among immigrants of many nationalities including refugees from racial pogroms in Poland and Russia. He saw the trade union as an agency in which all foreign-born could unite in spite of divergent interests and loyalties in other fields. Whatever their religious creed, their language, their political affiliation, all wage earners needed and wanted higher wages, shorter hours and protection against injustice. He did not advocate special privilege or indulgences for minority groups—only equal opportunity.

S. G. used the general strike in New Orleans to illustrate absence of the color line in trade unions. Negro draymen formed a union whose officers attempted to negotiate a contract with employers. The employers refused to talk with Negroes or make a contract with the draymen. S. G. with pride told the U.S. Industrial Commission in 1899:

Organized labor of New Orleans went on a strike; every machinist went on a strike; every printer went on a strike; no paper made its appearance; the men working in the gas houses went on a strike and there was no illumination that night; the bakers went on a strike, and all other white workers went on a strike for the purpose of securing recognition of the colored workmen.*

He added:

If there is any union of labor that says anything or takes any action regarding the colored man of the South it is not because of his color; it is because he has as an individual or because they have generally in that trade so conducted themselves as to be a

* Testimony, U.S. Industrial Commission, Washington, D.C., April 18, 1899.

continuous convenient whip placed in the hands of the employer to cow the white men and to compel them to accept abject conditions of labor.*

We have more than 700 volunteer organizers and a number of organizers under salary, among which are several who are devoting their time exclusively to the organization of the colored workers. This certainly should indicate not only our desire and interest, but also the work which is being accomplished . . .

The real difficulty in the matter is that the colored workers have allowed themselves to be used with too frequent telling effect by their employers as to injure the cause and interests of themselves as well as of the white workers. They have too often allowed themselves to be regarded as "cheap men," and all realize that "cheap men" are an impediment to the attainment of the workers' just rights, and the progress of civilization.*

He also protested undercutting of union cigarmakers' standards by coolie immigration workers and backed California cigarmakers in securing an exclusion act barring Chinese coolies from entrance to our country.

Never in the history of the world have Chinese gone to any country in any considerable numbers without one of two things occurring—first, that the Chinaman has dominated, or he has been driven out by force. The Chinaman is a cheap man.*

The American people do not object to the Chinese because they are Chinese; they know from their own experience, as well as from the experience of ages of the people of other countries, that the Chinese coolies and laborers can not assimilate with our race; that their civilization, and ours as well, can not co-exist; that the physical conditions, the standard of life, the progress of our people, will not only be endangered but undermined and destroyed.*

When alien-contract exclusion principles for dealing with immigration problems proved inadequate, S. G. regretfully, because he had been an immigrant under the open system, advised the literacy test to assure ability to participate in American life.

* Ibid.
* American Federationist, April 1901.
* Conference on Immigration, National Civic Federation, New York, December 1905.
* President's Report, Convention Proceedings, 1906.

Even when induced immigration stimulated by contracts between large industries and steamship companies to supply them annually with new immigrants became a menace to American institutions, S. G. was still anxious to maintain this country as a haven for the poor and oppressed of all nationalities and urged standards of selection that would maintain that tradition.

Mr. Gompers advocated the principle—no union discrimination because of sex. He gave strong backing to the woman suffrage movement and endorsed the principle of equal pay for equal work. As a practical measure he urged organization of working women in trade unions. With respect to women he digressed again from his general principle—"by workers, for workers, through workers"—and promoted the Women's Trade Union League modeled after a similar English organization, conditional on compliance with Federation policies. He warned the right to vote did not settle industrial problems, which must be worked out in the same way as men's problems.

The right to vote does not mean that women will necessarily have work. Equal suffrage does not necessarily mean equal pay for equal work. These industrial problems women will work out only when through organization they have industrial power and influence that will enable them to secure higher wages, shorter hours and better working conditions. The relations between suffrage and industrial betterment must not be confused. It is a matter of justice that there should be equal pay for equal work. The ballot will help but will not necessarily bring this about. It will result only from the intelligent self-interested activity on the part of the women.*

There is no difference in the industrial problems and difficulties which confront women from those which confront men. The fundamental principles which underlie all efforts of women to establish their rights and industrial justice are those which underlie efforts of men. Men and women united can work out a general plan for the economic welfare of all, and together they can enforce their demands and ideals. Divided in their efforts, or working along separate plans, there must be some degree of conflict and wasted activity.*

* Press statement, August 1915.
* American Federationist, March 1916, pp. 200–2.

He believed the first responsibility of the married woman was to her home and that her husband's wages through union standards should cover the costs.

I contend that the wife or mother, attending to the duties of the home, makes the greatest contribution to the support of the family. The honor, glory, and happiness that comes from a beloved wife and the holiness of motherhood are a contribution to the support and future welfare of the family that our common humanity does not yet fully appreciate . . .

There is no reason why all the opportunities for the development of the best that women can do should be denied her, either in the home or elsewhere. I entertain no doubt but that from the constant better opportunity resultant from the larger earning power of the husband the wife will, apart from performing her natural household duties, perform that work which is most pleasurable for her, contributing to the beautifying of her home and surroundings.*

Wife, children, home, are at the heart of his union planning and purpose, as they are also at the heart of individual and national life.

* American Federationist, January 1906.

14. Opposition to Regimentation

Socialists proposed political action and legislative procedure where S. G. proposed economic power and procedures, voluntary agencies resting upon individual responsibility and freedom. Socialists would substitute political party government with police enforcement for voluntarism through voluntarily associated agencies regulating relationships through contracts and maintaining order by mutual consent.

Karl Laurrell taught Gompers that Socialism aimed at changing our basic institutions, substituting government ownership for private property, and that it was essentially a revolutionary cause not adapted to problems and purposes of trade unionists who must deal with existing institutions and conditions. Socialists must first concentrate on building up their machinery for control and then institute the new commonwealth before workers would make substantial progress. It was a subject for debate in which slogans, catchy phrases, clever anecdotes, could be used effectively and devastatingly. In his public and labor speeches, S. G. condemned, ridiculed and vanquished the Socialists by his ability to coin phrases and epithets. However, he also presented fundamental reasons for his opposition based upon the priority he assigned to the right of each individual to personal freedom and the development of his responsible personality. These rights he thought were of higher importance than security.

He dealt with individual Socialists, "boring from within" or infiltration, by educating trade unionists in the fallacies of Socialism and to detect and answer their proposals. In the early conventions, Socialist resolutions, the committee reports dealing with them and the recurring debate were an annual event. S. G. always made the closing speech. His most quoted summary closed the 1903 convention debate:

I want to tell you Socialists that I have studied your philosophy; read your works upon economics, and not the meanest of them; studied your standard works, both in English and German—have not only read them, but studied them. I have heard your orators and watched the work of your movement the world over. I have kept close watch upon your doctrines for thirty years; have been closely associated with many of you, and know how you think and what you propose. I know, too, what you have up your sleeve. And I want to say that I am entirely at variance with your philosophy. I declare it to you, I am not only at variance with your doctrines, but with your philosophy.

Economically, you are unsound; socially, you are wrong*; industrially, you are an impossibility.**

This withering blast at Socialists closed the debate in the Boston Convention on the report of the Committee on Resolutions to non-concur in the usual line of battle of resolutions to commit the American Federation of Labor to socialism (communism) in some form. It has been repeated again and again by loyal trade unionists and appreciatively quoted by officials responsible for maintaining trade unionism against the manifold subtle proposals of these party well-doers and the never flagging machinations of party members who sought to gain by intrigue what they could not do in open contest. The headquarters of the International Workingmen's Association founded by Karl Marx and Friedrich Engels when it was forced to leave Europe, went to London in 1864 and then was shipped to the United States for disintegration and interment. Socialists-communists gathered about the remains, as did refugee revolutionaries of the world. Various American Socialist organizations formed but did not find friendly soil.

S. G. was thoroughly familiar with the techniques and amoral strategy of the communist-socialist advocates who fought his policies and organized dual movements to wreck his work. Undoubtedly S. G. and the trade unionists who

---

* John Frey, who was so much impressed by this speech that he took notes, says Mr. Gompers used the word "unsafe" instead of "wrong" which appears in the text.

** Statement, 1903 Convention Proceedings.

taught and advised him were the potent factor in the failure of Socialism to gain greater hold in the labor movement. Marxian Socialist-Communism or collectivism, like Lenin-Stalin Communism, found its greatest success in the United States among the "intellectuals" and was most promoted consciously or unconsciously by instructors in colleges and universities.

With Gompers' vehement emotional temperament and intellectual acuteness in discerning inequities and injustice he would seem like a person custom-made for socialism. There was an old legend that he early had a party card. This he as vehemently denied as the Socialists persistently repeated. Whether there were conclusive facts for or against in this debate is not so important as that S. G. was made immune to the virus by two remarkable teachers: Karl Ferdinand Laurrell—a Swedish trade unionist to whom he dedicated his autobiography and Adolph Strasser—an Austrian Jew. Laurrell was first a seaman, then learned cigarmaking in Copenhagen and later went to Hamburg where, together with his work in the International Workingmen's Association, he became familiar with German economic thought. He left Europe after participating in a demonstration before the royal palace in Copenhagen. He went to New York where he found employment in the cigarmaking shop of David Hirsch—a German Jewish "exile." Hirsch had been directed to leave Hamburg because of revolutionary activity. His shop was a sort of receiving center for other German "exiles." There also S. G. met Adolph Strasser, a Viennese (or Hungarian?) whose past was a mystery. S. G. said no one definitely knew his background and that he obviously had been something else than a wage-earner for his training, clothing and intellectual capacities suggested at least a well-to-do family. These exiles transmitted a goodly heritage to the American labor movement.

Laurrell safe-guarded Gompers from Socialism by teaching him the paramount importance of developing economic power through the trade union using that power to gain higher wages and shorter hours—the two most vital, most revolutionizing forces that come into the lives of workers and their families. Laurrell drilled Gompers in the principles and theory necessary to make trade unions practical, stabilized agencies for service to workingmen. Strasser and Gompers first worked in developing the structure and the operation of cigarmakers local and national unions and later the structure and operational procedure of the American Federation of Labor. It seems a bit curious that two such able and knowledgeable men should have come to New York to that particular cigar shop at just the right time in Gompers' career. The result of the teaching of these two men and their generosity in sharing experiences was the "pure and simple trade unionism" with which he implemented his philosophy of voluntarism as well as that philosophy itself, supplemented by his political action program, partisan not to a party but to the principles of equal rights and freedom for all citizens.

In all the long years when S. G. gloried in his fight against Socialism and yielded no ground to their proposals he used their proposals as occasions for detailed discussion which educated other trade unionists in the arguments for and against socialism and in explaining why economic methods and power were more effective in bringing betterment to workers and higher standards of living than political. There is a fascination about the game of politics that attracts the unwary and Gompers tried to fore-arm trade unionists so that they might be able to discern the genuine from the spurious. Some of the warfare required backbone as well as a clear head such as the loathsome propaganda of the Socialist Trades and Labor Alliance with its effort to malign Gompers and undermine the Federation; the American Labor Union; the Industrial Workers of the World; the Western Labor Union; and then the Communist Party and its determination to destroy free institutions including free enterprise and free labor unions. The Socialist Party was continuously gnawing at Gompers' non-partisan political action in the hope difficulties would force him to yield in his opposition to forming a labor party. But Gompers was aware of the impediments attaching to a political party. These included if successful problems attaching to patronage, decisions with respect to the forces of the invisible government and current political

blackmail of which he was conscious, divisive factors inherent in decisions on national policies other than labor,
etc. He was fully aware of the growing political power of
the underworld which gained such impetus during the
period of the prohibition amendment. Through his masonic
and other personal connections he had information through
other powerful international forces and thereby secured
information useful for his guidance.

In 1915—First World War—the Socialists made two
major onslaughts against S. G.'s leadership—a resolution
in the A. F. of L. Convention to secure a Federal eight-
hour law covering private industry and a Congressional
inquiry into health insurance to indicate the form of legislative provisions. Perhaps the national party here was
cooperating with international officials or agencies in an
effort to discredit S. G.'s war activity. The resolution was
sponsored by John Fitzpatrick, a lovable Irish horse-shoer
who for years was the heart of the Chicago Federation of
Labor. That Fitzpatrick was known throughout the United
States as a devoted trade unionist and the soul of honesty
gave greater appeal to the resolution. He was then working closely with W. Z. Foster on organizing packing-house
and steel workers around Chicago. Foster at that time
was not known as a Moscow agent. S. G. somehow
got wind of the move and began marshalling his forces
and arguments. The Convention met that year in San Francisco and was prolonged by much discussion, so that by
general agreement the election of officers, usually the last
order of business, was advanced a few days to enable union
officials to go East to take care of urgent matters.
That was one of the few times S. G. seemed worried about
convention decision on basic policy. The debate was long
and heated. Mr. Gompers closed it as usual. His policy
was confirmed as the Convention endorsed the report of the
Resolutions Committee declaring that one of Labor's greatest earlier victories was the winning of industrial freedom
through repeal of laws fixing terms and conditions of work.

The Socialist group in New York City had succeeded
in electing a Socialist as a member of the House of Representatives. A number of Socialists and welfare workers

saw in this situation an opportunity to promote health insurance which Mr. Gompers had consistently opposed because it meant regimentation and weakening of wage-earners' independence by making them dependent on the State, as Bismarck had done in Germany, and thereby impeding policy to raise wages continuously by economic power so that wage-earners could pay for their own medical services. That he had not been consulted in advance on the legislation he knew was part of the Socialist plan to take him unawares and therefore at a disadvantage. He was out of Washington on official business when the hearings began. Only advocates of the bill appeared and the hearing was proceeding enthusiastically with a most favorable press.

His Executive Council was meeting in Washington and he reported the situation to them to have specific official backing and then telephoned the committee in charge of the hearing, stating dates when he could appear before them. On the appointed day, he "entered" the committee room bristling with offended dignity and recovered control of labor policies. He, the head of the most representative labor organization in the country, had not been consulted in advance although his organization was vitally concerned! His sense of drama and his use of his powerful voice conveyed to those in control their mistake in trying to circumvent him and side-track Labor upon a matter in which Labor had a right to control. After he finished his criticism of committee deportment, lack of courtesy and disregard for customary procedure, he vigorously concentrated on the bill and line by line sharply criticized words and substance until he made the drafters look like amateurs. Then he read a substitute bill—a proposal for health insurance on a voluntary basis with substantial benefits. Then he began his argument in which he used his most powerful incisive vocabulary. He loved and respected the English language and knew how to use it effectively.

He explained the trade union movement as guided by the ideal of human freedom as a constructive development and growth and he read data showing progress in shorter hours, higher wages and longer life. These things were the basis of progress for better health, he maintained, as he indicated the hardships and obstacles that had been overcome. Workers had been making substantial progress through their own agencies—trade unions. Led by Socialists, the professional welfare workers and intellectuals proposed to slow this progress by a dangerous experiment,—like German health insurance.

He quoted Frederick Howe's statement:

Germany has so strengthened the state as to have devitalized the individual.*

Health insurance by legislation was instituted in Germany by Chancellor Bismarck as an integral force in developing the Federal German Reich into which he was welding various independent German states. Health insurance legislation and administration affecting directly the work and home lives of all German workers brought them under control by the Kaiser and his agents and gave them a stake in the fortunes of the Reich. Samuel Gompers declared:

Doing for people what they can and ought to do for themselves is a dangerous experiment. In the last analysis the welfare of the workers depends upon their own initiative. Whatever is done under the guise of philanthropy or social morality which in any way lessens initiative is the greatest crime that can be committed against the toilers. Let social busy-bodies and professional "public morals experts" in their fads reflect upon the perils they rashly invite under this pretense of social welfare.*

Then he again explained to the committee the guiding philosophy of trade unionism—the philosophy of conservatives who believe in human freedom. Health was not an isolated problem or goal but was conditioned by the whole framework of wage-earner existence. The development of the trade union organization which struck directly at causes of sickness and ill health—long hours, sub-standard living conditions, worry due to injustice and insecurity, was the primary agency for promoting workers' health by steadily promoting a living wage and work hours to serve their mental and physical needs.

* American Federationist, May 1916, p. 351.
* From pamphlet, The Workers and the Eight-Hour Work-day, 1915.

He declared:

The workers of America adhere to voluntary institutions in preference to compulsory systems which are held to be not only impractical but a menace to their rights, welfare and their liberty. Health insurance legislation affects wage earners directly. Compulsory institutions will make changes not only in relations of work but in their private lives, particularly a compulsory system affecting health, for good health is not concerned merely with time and conditions under which work is performed. It is affected by home conditions, social relations, and all of those things that go to make up the happiness or the desolation of life.

To delegate to the government or to employers the right and the power to make compulsory visitations under guise of health conditions of the workers is to permit those agencies to have a right to interfere in the most private matters of life. It is, indeed, a very grave issue for workers. They are justified in demanding that every other voluntary method be given the fullest opportunity before compulsory methods are even considered, much less adopted.

The trade unionists who have considered the problem and expressed an opinion have advised against such compulsory institutions.

Compulsory sickness insurance for workers is based upon the theory that they are unable to look after their own interests and the state must interpose its authority and wisdom and assume the relation of parent or guardian.

There is something in the very suggestion of this relationship and this policy that is repugnant to free-born citizens. Because it is at variance with our concepts of voluntary institutions and freedom for individuals, Labor questions its wisdom.*

He appeared throughout the hearing deeply angered and pained by their incredible stupidity in not being able to distinguish between change and progress, and in their attempt to trick the American public and Labor into a plan to substitute the police state for free institutions with their evolution and growth. By charge of things undone and things done wrongly he had the Socialists startled and apologetic.

The whole scheme, the whole fault, the whole philosophy represented by Dr. Rubinow officially before this committee and by Mr. London as a representative of his political party, contem-

* American Federationist, April 1916, p. 270.

plate not individual development, not opportunity for initiative, for voluntary action, but regulation by the State. These people want to have laws enacted to make the other people conform to their concepts and recipes out of number . . .

. . . the American trade union movement, the A. F. of L., refuses to yield to any group one inch of the field of activity in the interests of the working people. The advocates of government regulation may fight for it, but they will find a stout contender against them in each human activity. They have been unable to control the American trade union movement, and that is the great sumtotal of our offense.

The A. F. of L. and the American trade union movement is the most effective militant, beneficent labor movement, freer from governmental interference, influence, or control, than any other labor movement in the whole world. It is because we are a labor movement, pure and simple, *per se,* a movement of wage-earners, for wage-earners, by wage-earners, that we incur the flippant, and sometimes the serious attacks and criticisms and subtle antagonism of the Socialist movement.*

Single handed he opposed the measure which had a popular appeal and succeeded in blocking action. It was a dramatic and memorable contest—soon obscured by the oncoming war. The intellectuals and welfare workers continued their propaganda—as did S. G. In 1917 he wrote:

Social insurance cannot remove or prevent poverty. It does not get at the causes of social injustice. The only agency that does get at the causes of poverty is the organized labor movement. Social insurance in its various phases of sickness insurance, unemployment insurance, death benefits, etc., only provides the means for tiding over an emergency. The labor movement aims at constructive results—higher wages, which mean better living for the worker and those dependent upon him; better homes, better clothing, better food, better opportunities and shorter hours of work, which mean relief from over-fatigue, time for recuperation, workers with better physical development and with sustained producing power. Better physical development is in itself an insurance against illness and a certain degree of unemployment. The short hour workmen with higher wages become better citizens; better able to take care of themselves . . .

* Gompers' statement, House Committee on Labor, H. J. Res. 159, April 11, 1916. American Federationist, May 1916, pp. 346–7.

Compulsory social insurance cannot be administered without exercising some control over wage-earners. This is the meat of the whole matter. Industrial freedom exists only when wage-earners have complete control over their labor power. To delegate control over their labor power to an outside agency takes away from the economic power of those wage-earners and creates another agency for power. Whoever has control of this new agency acquires some degree of control over the workers. There is nothing to guarantee control over that agency to the employed. It may also be controlled by employers. In other words, giving the government control over industrial relations creates a fulcrum which means great power for an unknown user.

Compulsory social insurance is in its essence undemocratic. The first step in establishing social insurance is to divide the people into two groups—those eligible for benefits and those considered capable to care for themselves. The division is based upon wage-earning capacity. This governmental regulation tends to fix the citizens of the country into classes, and a long established insurance system would tend to make these classes rigid.

There is in our country more voluntary social insurance than in any other country of the world.*

His final conclusion reflected the priority he gave to individual freedom in his hierarchy of values:

As I live, upon the honor of a man, and realizing the responsibility of my words, I would rather help in the inauguration of a revolution against compulsory insurance and the regulation than submit. As long as there is one spark of life in me, of my mentality, whatever that may be, of my spirit, I will help in crystallizing the spirit and sentiment of our workers against the attempt to enslave them by the well-meaning siren songs of philosophers, statisticians and politicians. We propose to work out our problems day after day, week after week, and year after year. We are not afraid.*

* American Federationist, January 1917.
* Testimony, House Labor Committee on social insurance, April, 1916.

15. Economic versus Legislative Methods

S. G. believed that economic problems had best be dealt with by economic agencies and economic procedures, and that transferring a problem to the political field solved no part of the economic problem but complicated solution and facilitated corruption in government. Such transfer would substitute substantive law for a private contract kept current by re-negotiation by the parties concerned; and control in the interests of a political party instead of control in the interests of employees and employers; recourse to courts instead of policing through management and workers, reinforced by lock-outs, strikes and boycotts. As he pointed out:

> Another difficulty with the legislative method is the diffusion of effort. There are comparatively few people interested in the matter, and yet the whole body politic must be interested, educated and roused to action.
>
> Contrast this with the simple, direct methods of economic action. Those workers who want the shorter workday know why they want it, and they want it so intensely that they are ready to fight for it. Forceful independent men and women, they assume the responsibility of their own welfare and make sacrifices to secure their rights. By agreement or by strike, they secure what they need, and because they have won it themselves they value it and maintain it. They are organized in such a way that they can give expression to their will and secure results in the most direct way possible.*

When workers and employers jointly determine standards, the workers concerned with production constitute part of the machinery for enforcement. When a law must be enforced the government organizes an administrative system outside the industry. Then both workers and employers have the added responsibility of checking on the administrators.

* American Federationist, March 1915.

100

He urged the development of order by industry to forestall its imposition by political government with, probably, a resulting bureaucracy:

Trade unionism, as an integral and ever functioning part of human society, has had its full share of tremendous experiences and it has not failed to observe the experiences of all other functional elements in society.

What we have observed is that the period ending with the beginning of the World War found political democracy in its fullest state of development, while the close of that period of overwhelming upheaval marked the opening of the period of intelligent demand and living need for industrial democracy. The close of the war marked for us a turning point in human relations and threw forth in bold relief the inadequacy of existing forms and institutions. Henceforth trade unionism has a larger message and a larger function in society. Henceforth the movement for the organization of the workers into trade unions has a deeper meaning than the mere organization of groups for the advancement of group interests, however vital that function may yet remain.

Henceforth the organization of the workers into trade unions must mean the conscious organization of one of the most vital functional elements for enlightened participation in a democracy of industry whose purpose must be the extension of freedom, the enfranchisement of the producer as such, the rescue of industry from chaos, profiteering and purely individual whim, including individual incapacity, and the rescue of industry also from the domination of incompetent political bodies.

The largest freedom of action, the freest play for individual initiative and genius in industry can not be had under the shadow of constant incompetent political interference, meddlesomeness and restriction.

Through the muddling conflict of groups who still find it impossible to come together in cooperation we must look to a future that must have its foundation upon cooperation and collaboration. The threat of state invasion of industrial life is real. Powerful groups of earnest and sincere persons constantly seek the extension of state suzerainty over purely industrial fields. Such ignorant encroachments as the Esch-Cummins Act, the Kansas Court of Industrial Relations and the Colorado Industrial Commission Act, each a blundering gesture of government acting under the spur of organized propaganda or of political appetite for power, are examples of what all industry has to fear. The continuing clamor for extension of state regulatory powers under the guise of reform and deliverance from evil, can but lead into greater confusion and more hopeless entanglements. Trade unionism must lead the way for true progress, even at the cost of being branded as reactionary by those who do but little save propound formulas based upon utopian thought and devoid of the benefit of experience and of any cognizance of our fundamental social structure, our industrial life or our national characteristics. We advocate organization of all wage earners and of all useful and productive elements.

We feel that we shall not labor the point if we review what we have repeatedly said and what all students know, that our national life today is becoming more and more industrial and that the decisions that most vitally affect the intimate daily lives of our people are the decisions that are made in industry, in the workshops and factories, in the mines and mills, in the commercial establishments, on the railroads and in the counting rooms. The decisions that caused more than five million workers to be for months without work were not decisions of Congress. The decisions that quickened the wheels and brought men and women back into service were not the decisions of Congress . . .

. . . The ruthless drive of purely individual aim and ambition has given America tremendous industrial giants. Great abuse has accompanied great achievement. But what is frequently overlooked is the fact that the ambition to build has been the driving force behind our most remarkable strides. The abuses, terrible and costly as they have been, have been largely coincidental.

The ambition to build must be saved . . .

. . . Industry alone has the competence and it must demonstrate that competence through organization. The organized functional elements in industry will find easy of solution those problems to which politicians now turn their attention in futility. Industry must organize to govern itself, to impose upon itself tasks and rules and to bring order into its own house. Industry must bring order to itself constructively, or it will have an order thrust upon it which would be demoralizing if not fatal. Our people can not live and thrive under the regime of bureaucracy that threatens unless industry solves its own problems . . .

. . . The operation of industry for the dominant purpose of producing private profits has led to a multitude of abuses. It has produced all of the evils of autocracy because it is autocratic. Every factor that enters into the sustenance or operation of industry must be safeguarded and its just reward assured, but there must be an end to final control by any single factor . . .

While we have no wish to offer unasked advice to those who

occupy any other field in our productive life, we feel that we may suggest that agriculture, the great life-giving twin of industry, must find its way through to orderliness and justice by adoption of substantially the same methods which we advocate for industry. We fail to find any opportunity for difference in principle.

During the past year the relations between industrial workers and productive agriculture have grown tremendously; understanding has been developed everywhere between those who give productive effort in these two great fields.

It is our hope that farmers will continue their work of organization and that we may have and give assistance in pushing forward the programs upon which we believe depends our future national well-being and safety.

We have sought to set forth a great goal—the goal of America's wage earners—and the salvation of the masses of our people and of our inspiring industrial supremacy. We covet life and the fuller development of life and we therefore demand in behalf of the masses of our people the only course that can make possible the satisfaction of our ambition, the achievement of our ideal and the preservation of our essential liberties. American industry dare not confess incompetence. We call upon all who have eyes to see to join us in a great crusade for industrial democracy as the means to a greater national and individual life and as the means to the preservation of the genius of our people. Industry is the bedrock of modern civilization. We must bring order through organization into that life or suffer it to fall under the domination of a state bureaucracy which must be destructive alike of freedom for the individual and of progress for industry as a whole.*

S. G. early learned the difficulties in getting good administration and recognized in administration by those outside industry the beginnings of a new despotism by those who "know best" what is good for others. He witnessed only the beginnings of administrative law in this country but had studied Europe, Australia and New Zealand. He advocated the association of direct representatives of private agencies concerned with governmental administrators as a necessary safeguard, as in the original Vocational Education Act.

In 1908 he urged citizens to look where they were

* 1923 Convention Proceedings, report prepared for the Executive Council, pp. 31–34; also pamphlet, "Industry's Manifest Duty."

drifting when courts were denying workers' rights which were inherently and naturally theirs.

He went on to spell out the dangerous trend:

> Ours is not the first republic in the world. There are older republics now in existence. There was that great republic of Rome, which went into decay. There are some who imagine that the republic of Rome went by the board overnight, that it was simply swept out of existence like a thunderbolt from a clear sky. In truth, for many and many years the process of disintegration went on; first, in the denial of a certain liberty or right to a certain portion of the people—for it is in the nature of things that as soon as the denial of rights is proceeded with in the one instance it is accompanied by the bestowal of extra privileges upon another class. So, by filching the liberties of the people, one by one; tranquilizing one and trying to satisfy others—by this process the very essentials of liberty, character, independence, thoughtfulness and manfulness were taken out of the hearts of the Roman people until a mere shell of the republic existed. The people of Rome no longer had any interest in the maintenance or the perpetuation of what was then called a republic. There was no incentive for its defense in the hearts and minds of the people, and, hence, no wonder that it fell an easy prey to a handful of invading barbarians.*

Mr. Gompers frequently quoted Junius: "Eternal vigilance is the price of liberty." Nor did he believe in control by an elite group:

> Class is no assurance of genius, ability or wisdom. No man is fit to control the lives of his fellows. The trade unions are the agencies through which wage-earners are working out their destinies and interposing a check upon the arbitrary power in industry. The spiritual effect of industrial freedom is of incalculable potency in determining the moral fibre of the nation.*

Intuition, collective subconscious, or whatever guided him often led him to react vigorously against a proposal even before going through the rationale but his reaction was generally sound.

He took comfort in knowing his policies were radical in the root meaning of the word and defended them against the charge of narrowness:

* Address at Chicago, Ill., May 1, 1908.
* American Federationist, November 1916.

"The narrowness of trade unionism." This phrase passes current, at full face value, in every camp and even in every grouplet of "intellectuals." In going the whole round of the "isms," sociological, ethical, legal, political, reformatory, played-out popular crazes, or "just out" social panaceas, one will hear expressed by the leaders a sentiment that the trade unionists are hide-bound conservatives—because they decline to rush in a body to take the magic medicine for social ills offered by the particular "ism" advocated by the critic in each particular case.

It is a fact that trade unionism in America moves on its own set and deliberate way. In so doing, it has outlived wave upon wave of hastily conceived so-called "broad" movements that were to reconstruct society in a single season. And it has sufficiently good cause for continuing its own reasoned-out course.*

When union members agreed upon new economic standards they had to determine whether to proceed by economic or political action:

To strengthen the state, as Frederick Howe says, is to devitalize the individual. I am not a pessimist. On the contrary, I believe I may justly call myself an optimist. I believe in people. I believe in the working people. I believe in their growing intelligence. I believe in their growing and persistent demand for better conditions, for a more rightful situation in the industrial, political and social affairs of this country and of the world. I have faith that the working people will better their condition far beyond that which it is today.

The position of the organized labor movement is not based upon misery and poverty, but upon the right of workers to a larger and a constantly growing share of the production, and they will work out these problems for themselves.*

He warned that legislative regulation grows in a chain process:

Now regulation of industrial relations is not a policy to be entered upon lightly—establishment of regulation for one type of relation necessitates regulating of another and then another, until finally all industrial life grows rigid with regulations . . .*

It is interesting that Gompers recognized so early that controls in the hands of government administrators

---

* President's report, Convention Proceedings, 1910.
* Congressional Committee, April 1916, Social Insurance.
* American Federationist, May 1915.

(appointed persons not directly responsive to political or economic opinion of voters) could become the source of the new despotism called bureaucracy which regulates important undertakings and handles huge amounts of the nation's wealth. Persons hedged about by civil service and planted in lower echelons can determine policies in effect and completely transform national institutions but are difficult to detect from the outside and remove through any security machinery so far devised. Dependence on informers strikes at the heart of government for the people and by the people with a devastation equal to that of the "termites" boring from within.

If the workers surrender control over working relations to legislative and administrative agents, they put their industrial liberty at the disposal of state agents. They strip themselves bare of means of defense—they can no longer defend themselves by the strike. To insure liberty and personal welfare, personal relations must be controlled only by those concerned.*

He believed that the main factor in maintaining human freedom and sustained progress was to keep alert and active the sense of individual responsibility together with opportunity for reward for initiative. In his period a comparatively small portion of workers were organized, trade unions were the shock troops able to establish new standards as a challenge to lower standards and unorganized workers. He himself felt a very definite responsibility for leadership of the unorganized and for making plain to them their opportunity lay through mobilization of their economic power. He told with pride how unorganized workers resisted wage cuts and how organized workers demanding higher rates assured employers they should increase production to pay for the increase.

His emphasis on use of economic methods instead of political was to assure control over policies and their administration directly to those concerned—an essential safeguard for individual freedom as well as free institutions. These were the conditions effective in furthering development of individual personalities. His trade union

* Pamphlet, "The Workers and the Eight-Hour Work-Day," 1915.

card was his guide in defeating major legislative proposals to control and regulate industries and their trades as well as compulsion for wage earners and their unions. Initiative must be preserved and encouraged by rewards and also made responsible by duties.

What Mr. Gompers hoped to prevent was the extension of political agencies and procedures to our economy and its problems. Political agents were to his mind developed and adapted to maintenance of social order and justice. What he hoped to accomplish through expansion and strengthening economic agencies and making them responsible, was responsible economic self-government for service to society. Economic self-government could move surely and directly for order, justice and efficiency in the economic field while extension of agencies and procedures of a different order would he feared lead to corruption and injustice—tyranny.

Voluntary agencies should operate economic institutions to make them most successful.

16. Labor's Competence as an Expert

In organizations of workers, by workers, for workers, S. G. discriminated sharply between their functions and those of other groups. This he did with respect to relations with employers and made no plans to interfere with their functions. He also recognized and sharply defined in his own thinking a field where cooperation would be richly rewarding to both producing workers and management—workers' experience in carrying out work orders, in using tools and work materials and in minimizing irregular work. Records of daily work experience and production—quantity and quality—followed by joint discussion of them, are procedures which focus attention on output, saving and economic use of materials, etc., and are reciprocally educational for lower production costs and higher quality production. He appreciated the value of developing such procedures and while he did not go into this extensively, he encouraged unions and management to do so. It was the main theme of a speech he made to an annual joint meeting of engineers, members of professional societies and responsible for labor relations and members of the Taylor Society held in the Engineers' Building in New York City. The idea of Samuel Gompers speaking in their building was a profound shock to some of the older members. That speech marked a step in the development of union-management cooperation.

He repeatedly affirmed labor's competence to determine its own policies and to know what was best for workers. Back in 1900 Mr. Gompers declared in an editorial:

We court the sympathetic aid of all, but we resent the attempt on the part of anyone not a wage worker to try to formulate the policy of the trade union movement.

"The emancipation of the workingmen must be achieved by the workingmen themselves" is an adage long ago recognized by the trade union movement; and if there are friends of our cause who are ineligible to membership in the trade unions and federal labor unions they will best demonstrate their sympathy by restraining their zeal to become members, and seeking by their supposed "superior" intelligence to fasten themselves upon the wage-workers' movement.

It may be true that some organizations at some time may fall into error; but it is better that we may err and learn by experience to avoid errors in the future than to have men whose interests are not identical with those of wage-workers direct the affairs of any of our labor organizations or of our general movement. The lesson thus far learned is that those other than wage-workers who seek membership in any of our organizations are either eaten up with their own vanity, or are self-seekers; and in either case it is destructive of the best interests of the workers. That from the counsel of many comes wisdom has long been recognized; and this wisdom is much more far-reaching in its influence for good than the supposed "superior" intelligence of either the professoriat, the business men, the theorists, the self-seekers, or the camp followers.*

He believed that persons with only academic disciplines should not dictate or determine union policies either through unions or through joint associations such as associations for labor legislation, etc. Lawyers, historians, economists, etc., could best help unions by technical counsel on implementing policies.

Let them return to their rightful work and acquiesce in the right of the labor movement to determine its own aims and policies and to organize and determine its own agencies and methods. Friendly constructive criticism is always welcome from any source, but the attempt to bulldoze or dominate the labor movement by others than the workers themselves will be resisted and resented to to the uttermost.*

The American labor movement has insisted upon the inherent dignity and ability of wage-earners, and has declared that they are intelligently competent to deal with their own affairs in a democratic fashion and to determine and formulate their own policies.

This long-established practice of American labor has provoked criticism and hostility on the part of that group who have sympathy but whose understanding of labor problems is academic. This group in other countries is called the "Intellectuals" and whenever given opportunity sought and seeks to dominate the labor movement.

* American Federationist, April 1900.
* American Federationist, May 1918.

The American labor movement has always been willing to accept the sympathetic cooperation of this group but has rejected all attempts at leadership or domination.

American workers insist that it is an essential application of democratic principles that they work out their own problems in their own way.*

Wisdom through work he saluted:

Many a plain, unschooled toiler in the ranks has an understanding of industrial conditions and forces that makes him an authority in that field. Though their terms may not be as nicely discriminating as those of the more conventional "economist," yet they know the realities of economics, what is practical, and what is merely theoretical and speculative. Culture does not consist wholly of book learning but is an attitude of mind, alert and aware of tendencies, able and willing to discern the real from the false, the enduring from the ephemeral. Nor would we discredit the work of the colleges, universities or social workers, nor undervalue the constructive work done by these agencies in helping to establish a more sympathetic, democratic understanding of social and industrial problems among all the people. It is because we deprecate any action or policy that detracts from the value of that work, that we deplore the assumption of censorship and arrogance on the part of any . . . The workers are not bugs to be examined under the lenses of a microscope by the "intellectuals" on a sociological slumming tour.*

From practical experience the wage earners know what policies will work in dealing with fellow-workers and what they can do with machines and materials.

Mr. Gompers recognized as operating in work experience what Karl Jung, as scientist, has identified and called the 'collective unconscious' or past experience of a group. Those with only academic training who did not realize this source of wisdom available to workers have not understood the American trade union movement which Samuel Gompers, with his intuitive instincts, founded and developed. They could read about the British and other national labor movements which turned to politics to supplement union strength, and understanding that field, call them the true progressives. Whereas they could not understand that Gompers' political action without a labor party was

* American Federationist, April 1918.
* American Federationist, February 1913.

rooted in a philosophy indigenous to United States of America institutions, fruitful in practical achievements and in conserving the unions themselves. Conservation of the union was always Samuel Gompers' final test as learned from Laurrell.

How wise he was in not entrusting leadership to intellectuals ought to be very plain even to intellectuals themselves now that the success of communist totalitarians in enlisting educators to service for their purposes has been exposed and explained.

"Pure and simple" trade unionism he conceived as an element in national life and development as well as an agency of service to its individual members.

Similarly, a trade union is not a machine fitted to the work of directly affecting all the civic, social and political changes necessary in society. But it first of all teaches the working classes the power of combination. Thenceforward it disciplines them, leads them to perform tasks that are possible, and permits the members of any of its affiliated bodies to attempt any form of social experiment which does not imperil the organization as a whole. The spirit of combination has the immediate effects of self-confidence for the democratic elements in the unions, of growth in the loyalty of workingman for workingman, of constant progressive achievement not confined to restricted limits. It is therefore a motive power continuously and variously applicable as the masses move forward and upward in their individual and collective development.*

He rated the "intellectuals" as he termed them as nuisances when they did not understand that experience in production develops its own competence and experts for which academic training is not a substitute or necessarily an aid and forgot that competency in one field does not mean competence in others.

The labor movement does not discount the service to civilization rendered by intellectual ability, but it is equally convinced that there is a vast supply of important fundamental knowledge that can be secured only through the slow accumulation of deductions from experience. In understanding and solving labor problems, information gained in the college lecture room or in doctrinaire discussions is not a substitute for the knowledge gained through solving labor problems in the shop, in the mill or in the mine.

* President's Report, 1910 Convention Proceedings.

. . . They (intellectuals) can act as advisers and the formulators of constructive plans and policies to be submitted to democratic consideration and decision by the workers themselves in the American labor movement.*

Samuel Gompers firmly believed in the rights of private ownership as well as its responsibilities. He believed private property was the basis of personal freedom and that employers maintaining private enterprise were a bulwark of strength to workers in maintaining free unions. He was unwavering in his faith in workers' ability to be self-governing and to become property owners. Employers as a whole learned to respect labor's right to self-determination.

S. G. and his advisers like John Frey and Andrew Furuseth described to their lawyers what practical objective they wanted to accomplish and what philosophy and principles directed their conclusions. They expected their lawyers to use their technical knowledge to tell them how best to express their objectives in legal terms and to represent them in courts accordingly. They did not expect or permit lawyers to determine controlling principles—thus they worked out procedures through which persons with technical competence should serve unions.

Because the "intellectuals" did the writing for publications and the teaching in schools and colleges, absence of understanding in technical literature worked for undervaluation of Samuel Gompers and the work of his heart and mind—the American Federation of Labor. The Socialists wanted to prove him without vision. As a matter of fact he did not want the restriction of a formal blue print or the "vision" that satisfied them but he wanted to be free to expand ideals as new possibilities emerged with each new achievement. The "intellectuals" neglected the workers' wisdom coming from practical experience and direct contacts with workers and human nature.

Emotionally S. G. was a revolutionary who rebelled at injustice; practically he wanted people to have more material comforts in the present with more opportunities for culture and leisure. He harnessed emotion to practicability.

As large scale production became increasingly wide-

* American Federationist, May 1918.

spread relations between employers and workers became more remote and impersonal, and employers in time discovered they did not have stable production staffs. Constant changes, replacements, continuous training of shifting workers added to production costs. Samuel Gompers commented on this in 1916 and pointed out that the basic fact about a worker was that he was a human being whose intellect and will should be coordinated in the responsibilities of production. It is this practical labor competence that makes them valuable counsellors in administration of labor matters and in advising on how policies will work. His point he illustrated thus:

When the economic advantages of avoiding changes in employees became apparent, employers began to investigate how many new employees were engaged during the year and why the old ones left. The reasons were found to be perfectly normal, human, because wage-earners are one hundred percent human. They have human aspirations and desires for self-betterment. They do not want to stay where they feel humiliated by injustice or by arbitrary authority determining their lives. They not only want fair conditions of work but they also want home life under pleasant surroundings.*

In that same speech he pointed to consideration of human problems as the key to development of cooperative relations:

Upon what principles must industry be organized to enable each plant to develop cooperation for increased production? This is the problem of personal relationships between managements and workers. Workers are not an impersonal factor in production as the term "labor" is usually interpreted—workers are human beings whose characteristics, impulses, ambitions are exactly like those of all other human beings.

Cooperation for production depends fundamentally upon good-will. Good-will cannot be forced—it must be earned. Cooperation of workers can be earned only by those employers who determine with workers the terms and conditions under which production is carried on. The day's work is just as big a thing in the life of the wage-earner as it is in the life of the employer. As a free man, he feels the same right to a voice in deciding conditions and determining them. The only way in which workers in industry may express and

* Address, Associated Advertising Clubs of the World, New Orleans, September 22, 1919.

defend their rights and interests is through organization and responsible representatives. This method insures a feeling of justice and constructive consideration of industrial problems. Organization leads to progress. Through orderly organization we open the way to consideration of difficulties and reduce the possibilities for industrial disruption.

In addition to providing for negotiations between managements and organizations of workers for the determination of those things which constitute industrial agreement, managements have a still further responsibility if they are to secure cooperation for increased production. Industrial health, safety and morale are vital. As these problems are primarily scientific, the management must look to specialists for information and suggestions.*

The labor expert is necessary to complement such specialists. He foreshadowed possible future development thus:

After all it is not so much the nature of the work done that lifts it above mere drudgery and transforms it into a calling as it is the attitude of the worker toward his work. There is a marked tendency in the educational and industrial world to foster a spirit and an understanding that shall give each confidence and professional pride in his particular job—whether it is grinding teeth or pins, collecting tickets or bond coupons, painting houses or pictures.

The ideal of modern education is to develop individual efficiency that shall enable the worker to take satisfaction in good work done with an understanding of its relation to social needs.*

* Address, Associated Advertising Clubs of the World, New Orleans, September 22, 1919.
* American Federationist, July 1913.

17. Non-Partisan Political Action

Political campaigns to secure specific legislation were customary among trade unionists long before a political program or a policy was formally defined and adopted. The graveyard of labor parties that had been formed but which failed to survive was arresting enough to discourage the Federation from that course. A tremendous effort was made in the Bryan free silver campaign to force S. G. to an active part in support of a Federation resolution endorsing that issue. S. G. reported to the Federation Convention:

The fact is, however, that our movement distinctly draws the line between political action in the interest of labor and party political action. This was more particularly emphasized at the last convention when it was declared as the settled policy of the trade-union movement that party political action of whatsoever kind shall have no place in the convention of the American Federation of Labor.*

Samuel Gompers observed in his annual report for 1898:

No one having any conception of the labor problems—the struggles of life—would for a moment entertain the notion, much less advise the workers, to abstain from the exercise of their political rights and their political power. On the contrary, trade union action on the surface is economic action, yet there is no act which the trade unions can take but which in its effect is political.*

An equally basic truth he wryly told his own cigar-makers union in 1906:

There are some men who cannot understand political action unless there is a party.*

* 1896 Convention Proceedings, Cincinnati, President Gompers' Report.
* Convention Proceedings, 1898.
* Address, Cigarmakers' Local 144, April 27, 1906.

115

Within the philosophy of this broad understanding he worked out a program of labor political action that would give trade unions relief from judicial and administrative situations that threatened the existence of trade unions. At the same time he safeguarded principles which had given trade unions strength, flexibility and unity.

Employers, "captains of industry" as they were called in the nineties, were a hardy group of pioneers with initiative and accustomed to direct action. The new world offered them opportunity as it did to wage-earners. It was a climate that stimulated effort, will and daring.

Trade unions began to grow as our country changed from an agricultural to a dominant industrial economy. Scientific and technical progress brought opportunity for greater development of natural resources. Growth of industries and factory production together with large scale production reduced opportunities for personal relationships between workers and employers, discouraging spontaneous cooperation in production. Impersonal relations with absence of contacts made for misunderstanding and ill-will. To correct these difficulties it became apparent workers must maintain unions in continuous operation and elect qualified agents to represent them collectively, in discussing production and shop problems with management.

As more stable trade unions developed effective economic power, and knowledge of how to use that power for the promotion of their own welfare, employers also organized for protection of their interests and welfare and some of them united for defense against "over-aggressiveness" on the part of unions in the Anti-Boycott Association, etc. They retained lawyers to find ways of curbing the growing power of unions and to handle their legislative proposals. Their lawyers in seeking ways to protect the employer's right to manage his business unrestricted by unions which asserted the right of wage-earners to consideration, found that equity courts could be induced to issue orders in labor disputes invoking the court's duty to protect property against damages and harm. Corporation lawyers requested judges to issue writs which ordered workers and unions to do and not to do things which the court signed often without reading. Some of the orders were subsequently revised to restore to workers their constitutional rights but the objective—timely restriction of effective union action—had been gained. Bill after bill was drafted and introduced in Congress seeking to restrain equity courts to their traditional function—protection of property. S. G. pointed out to legislators that the misuse of equity grew out of failure to distinguish between the products of labor and that fundamental human attribute—ability to produce or labor power. Products of labor are commodities and articles that flow into the commerce of our economy while labor power or ability to produce is inseparable from human beings. Commodities are material things while labor power is a spiritual attribute of individuals. Since individuals are free, employers contract with them to perform services in production but do not thereby acquire any property rights in their services or in the workers. Therefore equity courts have no jurisdiction in labor disputes, S. G. maintained. Judges cannot require performance of specific services in fulfillment of contracts but may award damages in case of destruction of property or punishment for violations of law.

When abuses of equity were climaxed by litigation under the Sherman Anti-Trust Law, asking for three-fold damages to business due to strike and boycott interference with their production and sales, attaching workers' homes and savings accounts to assure payment, it was obvious unions were headed for government by a judicial oligarchy and were stripped of constitutional rights. Corporation lawyers made friends with party politicians in Congress to block labor's efforts to get remedial legislation. The rules of the House of Representatives assured the Speaker party control of legislative action.

Applying the patterns of the founding fathers of our nation to Labor's needs, Samuel Gompers and the Executive Council of the American Federation of Labor drafted a Bill of Grievances setting forth their legislative wrongs which with all the drama at their command they submitted to the President, the Speaker of the House and the President of the Senate on March 21, 1906. This document ended with a program and a threat in these paragraphs:

We present these grievances to your attention because we have long, patiently, and in vain waited for redress. There is not any matter of which we have complained but for which we have in an honorable and lawful manner submitted remedies. The remedies for these grievances proposed by labor are in line with fundamental law, and with the progress and development made necessary by changed industrial conditions.

Labor brings these its grievances to your attention because you are the representatives responsible for legislation and for failure of legislation. The toilers come to you as your fellow-citizens who, by reason of their position in life, have not only with all other citizens an equal interest in our country, but the further interest of being the burden-bearers, the wage-earners of America. As Labor's representatives we ask you to redress these grievances, for it is in your power to do so.

Labor now appeals to you, and we trust that it may not be in vain. But if perchance you may not heed us, we shall appeal to the conscience and the support of our fellow-citizens.*

Congress adjourned without heed to the Federation's petition or its warning. Mr. Gompers had to make the next move.

He chose a bold course. The Maine elections opened the contest for continued Republican control of Congress. He selected a few staff men to accompany him and went into the second district which Congressman Littlefield had represented. Littlefield, as member of the House Judiciary Committee, had successfully blocked action on the anti-injunction legislation which the Federation requested. The Maine Federation of Labor requested him to visit Maine during the campaign. The press hailed Mr. Gompers' entrance into Maine with ridicule. "David attacks Goliath," "As Maine goes, so goes the rest of the election" they quoted. The cartoonists had a field day.

The politicians charged that the labor groups were outsiders invading a political jurisdiction in which they were not residents. So the Republican party sent in Joseph Cannon, William H. Taft, Senator Lodge, Senator Beveridge to counterbalance them.* In addition a message of support from the President of the United States. It was a contest that reverberated throughout the nation and moved industrial corporations to fiercer warfare on Labor.

* President's report, Convention Proceedings, 1906.
* American Federationist 1906, p. 798.

While this campaign did not prevent Littlefield's re-election it reduced his plurality over 80 percent—from 5419 to less than 1000—so that he did not seek re-election again and demonstrated the practicability of the method.

S. G.'s instructions to Maine voters were:

We will stand by our friends and administer a stinging rebuke to men or parties who are either indifferent, negligent or hostile and, whenever opportunity affords, secure the election of intelligent, honest, earnest trade unionists, with clear, unblemished, paid-up union cards in their possession.*

Meanwhile, harassment of unions by injunctions became so serious Samuel Gompers suggested to his Executive Council that the Federation make a test case in order to have a clear-cut case to submit to Congress and the Nation. The Molders' Union had asked the Federation to place the Bucks' Stove and Range Company on its unfair list asking unions to boycott its products nationally. The company responded by getting a Federal court to enjoin the officers of the Federation from speaking or writing about this case. To test the legality of this injunction S. G. continued to discuss the principles involved in public speeches and in published editorials. The court promptly charged him with contempt in violating the injunction. He as promptly replied he had the right of free speech.

When the Supreme Court of the United States in 1908 held the Sherman Anti-Trust Law applied to the Hatters' Union with triple damages and recourse against individual members, it was obvious the union plight was indeed desperate. In addition to other Federation lawyers Mr. Gompers retained Judge Alton B. Parker to argue constitutional issues involved.

The Federation set up a Committee on Political Action to submit demands for redress of grievances to both political party conventions and report back to unions the position each party incorporated in its party platform on labor's demands. These demands included the following paragraphs:

As the authorized representatives of the organized wage-earners of our country, we present to you in the most conservative and

* American Federationist, 1906, p. 293.

earnest manner that protest against the wrongs which they have to endure and some of the rights and relief to which they are justly entitled. There is not a wrong for which we seek redress, or a right to which we aspire, which does not or will not be equally shared by all the workers, by all the people.

While no Member of Congress or party can evade or avoid his or their own individual or party share of responsibility, we aver that the party in power must and will by labor and its sympathizers be held primarily responsible for the failure to give the prompt, full, and effective Congressional relief we know to be within its power.

We come to you not as political partisans, whether republicans, democrats, or other, but as representatives of the wage-workers of our country whose rights, interests and welfare have been jeopardized and flagrantly, woefully disregarded and neglected. We come to you because you are responsible for legislation, or the failure of legislation. If these, or new questions, are unsettled, and any other political party becomes responsible for legislation, we shall press home upon its representatives and hold them responsible, equally as we now must hold you.*

The national non-partisan labor political program was started. It was based on records from headquarters providing information on the position of the political party on key labor legislative issues and voting records of candidates on them. Local voting wage-earners were to question candidates as to their position on key issues and make this information available to union members. With this guidance workers were advised: Elect your friends and defeat your enemies.

S. G. injected no new organization but told the unions the facts of Labor's grievances, their petitions for redress and related the response of the party and the individual candidates on these matters which involved the existence of unions. He knew that American political traditions based party organization upon adherence to principles and included cross sections of voters of all social and geographical sectors and that no appeal along class bases would meet with success. Every individual voter treasures his privilege to use his vote to further his own and the country's best interests and resents interference with this right from any source. Any attempt to build political power by solidifying

* President's report, 1908 Convention Proceedings.

a single group he knew would be resented as undemocratic and out of line with American traditions. He met wage-earners' political needs through machinery that strengthened their confidence in the United States of America and so strengthened our political institutions. He was not opposing the Republican party candidates or advocating the election of Democratic candidates, but was seeking Democratic and Republican candidates pledged to give wage-earners relief from misuse of injunctions in labor disputes and application of anti-trust law to organizations of human beings. By reducing his political program to simplest terms, he prevented diversion of strength and interest from economic unity and union authority. "Elect Labor's friends and defeat its enemies" was his watchword.

As a stop gap a rider was attached to the Appropriations Bill for the Judiciary prohibiting use of any funds for proceedings against unions under the Anti-Trust Law. This was the first fruit of non-partisan politics.

Within a decade sixteen trade union members had been elected to the House of Representatives and one to the U.S. Senate. There had been a revolution in the attitude of Congress toward Labor proposals and a genuine effort to right their grievances. After this achievement for which the Democratic party was mainly responsible, it became increasingly difficult to maintain a strictly non-partisan attitude and procedure. Also Representatives became increasingly clever in evading roll-call voting—the record upon which the Federation based its classification of "friend or enemy." Also the personal records of helpful Republicans were clouded by less generous planks in their party platforms. This record did not disclose "unfriendly" manipulation of legislation within a committee to which it was referred for study and recommendation or how individuals voted in a voice vote.

Mr. Gompers met with some members of Congress who wanted to change the rules under which the House operated, which gave the Speaker almost absolute control over House committees and procedure, and by his helpfulness gained for Labor a new political significance and standing. Political leaders of all parties recognized that organized labor had entered a new field of national influence. Mr.

Gompers served the Federation and the United States by adhering strictly to conservative principles; maintenance of individual rights and freedom, the right to membership in private associations for promotion of personal welfare; ownership of private property as the basis of individual freedom, responsibility for the exercise of rights and the use of opportunities under established law and guided by moral principles. Since he believed the state should serve the people his policy was to help workers develop the means and the will to participate in guidance of the state. Since they had to convince voters of the justice, wisdom and expediency of their cause they relied on educational methods. Prompt disciplinary action against a few who tried to use union programs for other than officially decreed purposes increased the prestige of the non-partisan political policy and facilitated national agreement on social justice objectives.

Gompers' policies unified and integrated a numerically large group of citizens into the common machinery of our body politic, and thus minimized the development of demand for class political organization. A labor party invites the procedures of struggle for control to final domination—perhaps by totalitarian despots, political racketeers and those ambitious to build up various types of empire. Gompers was continually declaring to Labor that whatever permanent progress they made must rest on an educational foundation. He never promised to deliver the labor vote and realized he could not.

In 1908 S. G. stated to the annual convention:

The American labor movement is not partisan to a political party; it is partisan to a principle, the principle of equal rights and human freedom . . . Partisanship is exhibited by adherence to a party which refuses its endorsement (of our principles and policies), and non-partisanship consists in continued work for our principles regardless of what any political party may do.*

S. G. wrote in his official magazine:

Without forming a political party, without forming any new organizations, without additional expenditure of union funds, all except one of the demands contained in the Bill of Grievances have become the law of the land. The passage of the Immigration law,

---

* 1908 Convention Proceedings, p. 224. Words in parentheses added.

the last demand removed from the list, illustrates the distinctive
political power which organized labor has developed since 1906.
The proposal to restrict immigration was not a partisan measure.*

This was a crucial test of the principles of voluntarism.
While these changes were in the making, Mr. Gompers
had been sentenced to twelve months in jail for contempt of
court in the test case. In fixing the penalties, the Judge
charged the defendants with many misdeeds including law-
lessness. When given opportunity to address the court pro-
nouncing the sentence, he said:

Your Honor, I am not conscious at any time during my life
of having violated any law of the country or of the District in
which I live. I would not consciously violate a law now or at any time
during my whole life. It is not possible that under the circumstances
in which I am before Your Honor this morning, and after listening to
the opinion you have rendered, to either calmly or appropriately
express that which I have in mind to say. But, sir, I may be permitted to say this, that the freedom of speech and the freedom of the
press have not been granted to the people in order that they may
say the things which please, and which are based upon accepted
thought, but the right to say the things which displease, the right
to say the things which may convey the new and yet unexpected
thoughts, the right to say things, even though they do a wrong,
for one can not be guilty of giving utterance to any expression which
may do a wrong if he is by an injunction enjoined from so saying.
It will then devolve upon a judge upon the bench to determine in
advance a man's right to express his opinion in speech and in print.

There is much that I would like to say. I feel that I can not
say it now, but if Your Honor will permit me, I will say this.

Your honor has, in the course of your opinion accepted the
testimony adduced by the Buck's Stove & Range Company, accepted
it as evidence, and laid much stress upon the fact that the evidence
is not denied; and upon the failure to deny, I can readily understand
it may be accepted as having been admitted. But Your Honor will
see the situation. Suppose some citizen were brought before a court
charged with a crime, aye, even murder, and if advised and believing
that the judge sitting upon the bench would undertake to proceed
with the trial of the defendant without submitting such a case to a
jury, if the defendant were advised that the judge, in the
exercise of that function, violated the fundamental constitutionally
guaranteed rights of the citizen, hence that it was not requisite on

* American Federationist, March 1917.

his part to enter any defense, and that in the last analysis the higher courts would reverse the decision of the judges upon that ground, the citizen would therefore enter neither denial nor offer evidence in rebuttal to that presented by the prosecution.

It is true that the judge might hold that there being no denial of the testimony presented against him, therefore he would hold the charge as proved; yet, as a matter of fact, it may prove nothing of the kind, even though it may be before the Court.

I may say, Your Honor, that this is a struggle of the working people of our country, a struggle for rights. The labor movement does not presume to be a higher tribunal than the courts or the other branches of the government of our country, and the language quoted by the counsel for the Buck's Stove & Range Company, which I am very glad to have the opportunity of explaining, the language accepted by Your Honor in your opinion in regard to the A.F. of L. Conventions being the highest tribunal in the realms of labor, was not, either in my mind, or in the mind of any man that heard that report read, to apply to anything in which the rights of others outside of the labor movement were concerned. It was just that in the A.F. of L. convention some question as to jurisdiction, as to internal strife, and disputes, between these organizations, that in so far as these contests were concerned the decisions reached by the convention of the A.F. of L. should be received by all concerned as determining their contentions.

Yes, sir, it is a great struggle, it is a struggle of ages, a struggle of the men of labor to throw off some of the burdens which have been heaped upon them, to abolish some of the wrongs which they have too long borne, and to secure some of the rights too long denied.

If men must suffer because they dare speak for the masses of our country, if men must suffer because they have raised their voices to meet the bitter antagonism of sordid greed, which would even grind the children into the dust to coin dollars, and meeting with the same bitter antagonism that we do in every effort we make before the courts, before the Legislatures of our states, or before the Congress of our country, if men must urge this gradual rational development then they must bear the consequences.

That which Your Honor has quoted and criticized and denounced in us, in the exercise of our duties to our fellows in our own country is now the statute law of Great Britain, passed by the Parliament of that country less than two years ago. If in monarchical England these rights can be accorded to the working people, these subjects of the monarch, they ought not to be denied to the theoretically at least, free citizens of a republic.

In this struggle men have suffered. Better men have suffered than I. It is true that I do not believe that there is a man alive who would chafe more under restraint of his liberty than I would, but if I can not discuss grave problems, great questions in which the people of our country are interested, if a speech made by me on the public rostrum during a political campaign after the close of the taking of testimony in this case, if the speeches in furtherance of great principle, of a great right are to be held against me, I shall not only have to but I shall be willing to bear the consequences.

I say this to you, Your Honor, I would not have you to believe me to be a man of defiant character, in disposition, in conduct. Those who know me, and know me best, know that that is not my make-up; but in the pursuit of honest convictions, conscious of having violated no law, and in furtherance of the common interests of my fellow-men, I shall not only have to, but be willing to, submit to whatever sentence Your Honor may impose.*

The case was appealed to the Supreme Court but meanwhile he lived for years under the discomfort of that sentence. In 1914 the case was dismissed as moot without passing upon the principles involved, because an adjustment of the controversy had been made.

As he stated in 1917—

One great advantage of this (political) policy that the A.F. of L. has pursued is that it has in no way hampered or detracted from the economic power or effectiveness of the trade unions. Non-partisan political activity does not subordinate the economic interests of trade unionists to partisan interests but our political policy has made our economic influence, our economic needs, our economic welfare of paramount importance. The paramount issue of our political campaign was the enactment into law of legislation that would assure the legal right to organize and secure for labor organizations the legal right to perform those activities necessary to carry out the purposes of economic organizations.*

The purpose of the Federation's non-partisan political action was to secure, through the state, laws ensuring justice for wage-earners and their enforcement. The state is the agent of the people and should serve them. Mr. Gompers recognized that the state subject to law was the final authority in legal and political matters and was responsible for enacting such regulations as were necessary and for enforcing them.

* American Federationist, Jan.–Feb. 1909.
* American Federationist, February 1917.

18. Trusts and the Labor Power of a Human Being

Two of the most serious legal problems of trade unions with which S. G. contended were the use of injunctions in labor disputes and suits under the anti-trust law to curb or stop trade union activity. Equity law authorized judges to issue restraining orders to protect property against immanent damage. Persons who violated such orders were held to be guilty until they proved their innocence. A large body of judicial law developed out of repeated use of the injunction in labor disputes and precedents developed therefrom. Frequently the employers' lawyers hurriedly wrote the order submitted to the judge with the statement irreparable damage to property was imminent, which resulted in a temporary-or-longer denial of fundamental rights to workers concerned. As time is of the essence in labor disputes and revision of injunctions could not compensate for losses due to previous errors, injunction procedure did much to undermine Labor's faith in the integrity of the judiciary. Irresponsibility of judges became a frequent charge which resulted in demands for the election of judges.

That which the injunction sought to regulate or curb was, Mr. Gompers contended, the worker's labor power—an attribute of free human beings. The individual could not be in part free and also subject to control by a political or other agency. Therefore injunctions should not be issued against unions which consist of human beings and are not of the same order as property. In fact, ownership of property is a personal right resulting from personal thrift, production or inheritance.

In 1890 Mr. Gompers was in Washington during early discussion of anti-trust legislation. He listened to representatives of various groups and thought he caught purposes and intent. He interviewed a number of Senators including George, Hoar, Stewart, Morgan and others and urged that exemptions be specifically included in the bill exempting wage-earner and farmer organizations from its application. He thought they as individuals agreed to the wisdom of his proposal but the bill reported to the Senate did not contain the proviso he urged. He did not believe the legislation could correct the costs and abuses of trusts or that legislation was the way to accomplish those ends.

Our modern plan of production, which for brevity and convenience we call the trust system, is the most perfect yet attained. We do not, however, mean to imply by this that the individuals who form trusts, who manipulate them, who profit by them, are logically and inevitably right in many of the methods they employ or the lengths to which they go. Neither do we concede the argument that these individuals who form and manage trusts are so superior a class of beings that they are entitled to the enormous largesse which many of them claim from the profits of economical production. Quite the contrary is the fact. Much of the protest against trust methods is justly and legitimately based on the fact that trust promoters, managers, and owners seize and keep for themselves a far greater share of the profits of modern production and distribution than that to which they are entitled . . .

Many of these gentlemen are merely fortunate accidents in the crystallization of a new era. They too, often, forget that they are bound to give accounting, to do justice to that greater force which makes industry possible—the people—in their two capacities, as producers and consumers . . .

It is only fair to say that the greatest and most enlightened combinations of capital in industry have not seriously questioned the right and, indeed, the advisability of organizations among employees. There is economy of time and power and means of placing responsibility in "collective bargaining" with employees which bring the best results for the benefit of all.

Organized labor has less difficulty in dealing with large firms and corporations today than with many individual employers or small firms.*

Trusts of that time had not reached present monolithic proportions and concentration nor had they developed controlling inter-relations with the U.S. Government administrative agencies and political parties as well as trade between nations. The consolidation of economic and politi-

* Address, Chicago Conference on Trusts, October 1907.

cal controls, together with the military, which provides totalitarian power, was yet in the future.

The abuses of methods and functions by those controlling big industry are serious problems, he said, but not hopeless:

> In intelligent and associated use of the powers of the many will be found the solution. Disorganized and violent denunciation is more harmful than helpful. Constructive and associated effort must check and correct the abuses which have grown so rapidly in this era of concentrated methods of production and distribution.
>
> The wage-workers of the country are setting an example in this respect. Their efforts will be successful in proportion to the unity of their effort and the thoroughness with which the people at large realize that the masses are one in interest and have unlimited power to check aggression, if they but assert their rights and their powers and use them constructively, intelligently, and with unswerving persistence.*

So prophesied, in 1907, this old pioneer who had watched the transition from hand to mass production with tools operated by electric power. He still saw free men able to possess their souls if they were persistent in assuming responsibility for their own welfare.

Strikes, boycotts and similar control of their economic power by wage-earners would, he anticipated, be held as restraint of interstate commerce under the Sherman Act and liable to triple damages and even dissolution of unions. This latter happened to the Danbury Hatters Union when the modest homes and savings of individual union members were seized to pay damages which a judge awarded the company against which a strike and boycott were waged. These two problems which threatened union development and progress convinced Samuel Gompers the Federation's non-partisan political action must be made a major purpose.

Bills were drafted to regulate the use of injunctions in labor disputes and to end the application of anti-trust law to unions. Mr. Gompers did not (in his words) "join the hue and cry" against trusts for he thought large scale production was a natural and beneficial development. So when Congress in 1913 reviewed anti-trust law and abuses

* Ibid.

of equity power, his concern was for those sections which dealt with these two problems which concerned "life not property." He told the Senate Committee:

. . . Under certain circumstances, by governmental expediency or necessity, a man may be alienated from his property. Government may take it, under the right of eminent domain, and compensate him for it; or it may confiscate it for the safety of the Government or for the good of society or for the protection of life. But the right of man is in himself, and can not be alienated from him without alienating his existence from himself. You can not separate the rights of man from himself, from the person, from the flesh, from the body, from the soul. The right to ownership of one's self—you can not deprive me of my power of my government of myself, in my own labor and labor power, without controlling my body. I can not dispose of my labor power without disposing of that part of my body and soul and breath. Fundamentally, the basis upon which the injunctions have been issued is that the employer has so much invested in plant, in machinery, in material, and that because of that he has a right of property or property right, in so much of the labor power of a number of workmen, in order that he may carry on his business uninterruptedly and profitably. We hold that an employer has no such right. . . .

I am free to say to you, and I will stand by it, I hold, and I have said, that when an injunction undertakes to violate the constitutional rights guaranteed to me as a citizen I am going to assert my rights as a citizen to test the question and to take the consequences. . . .

The effort of the attorneys for the employers' associations . . . all of their injunctions are intended to be a curb upon the rights of the workers to exercise their constitutional rights to own themselves, to agree among themselves for the protection of their persons, their rights, and their interests against the aggression of the modern captains of industry.[*]

When the bill was under discussion in the Senate in 1914, he asked Senator Cummings to propose the following for insertion in the labor section:

The labor power of a human being is not a commodity or article of commerce.

Formulation of this basic principle was a long time

[*] 62d Congress, U.S. Senate Committee on the Judiciary, subcommittee hearings on Limiting Federal Injunctions, H.R. 23635, January 6, 1913, pp. 57 and 58.

germinating in Gompers' mind until it crystallized in the form in which it was added to the labor sections of the Clayton Anti-Trust Act. From the time of his 1890 trip to Washington when he learned of the proposal for anti-trust legislation he quickly saw the implicit complications for unions and began studying the problem. He had many long talks with his advisers, especially Andrew Furuseth —the Viking seaman whose life was dedicated to a struggle to "free the seamen, the last of the bondsmen."

He seems to have gotten his first clue to the formulation of the principle from a French workingman. A member of a French Commission (about 1850) examining a workman told him that labor was merely merchandise. The workman replied:

> If merchandise is not sold at one certain time it can be sold at another, while if I do not sell my labor it is lost for all the world as well as myself; and as society lives only upon the results of labor, society is poorer to the whole extent of that which I have failed to produce.*

Gompers mulled this reply over many years. In 1907 he had made this progress in his thinking:

> Trusts consist of organizations for the control of the products of labor. Laborers have not a product for sale. They possess their labor power; that is, their power to produce. Certainly there can not be a trust in anything which has not been produced. Hence, for this if for no other potent reason, it is economically unsound as well as it is untrue to designate organizations of labor as trusts.*

Finally the principle became clarified in his mind in the clear simple form in which he submitted it to Senator Cummings. Later he submitted this declaration to the International Labor Commission for inclusion in the labor section of the Versailles Treaty. It was included in the Commission's draft submitted to the Peace Conference and approved by the Conference. The drafting committee responsible for "harmony" of language in the whole document inserted the word "merely" after "not." The result

---

* Address, International Labor Congress, Chicago, September 1893.
* American Federationist, November 1907.

was division of United States labor support for ratification of the Treaty.

As Samuel Gompers observed:

The far-reaching revolutionary significance of that declaration is not fully grasped by all. It sweeps away legal precedents and legal philosophy that have served to impede Labor's efforts to rid itself of the conditions and relations that existed when human workers were born slaves and held as slaves.*

The labor sections of the Clayton Anti-trust Act tried to define and restrict the use of injunctions in labor disputes and were not effective in removing abuses. Abuses ended only after the Norris-LaGuardia Act of 1932 based on the principles he sponsored simply directed Federal Courts not to issue injunctions in cases of labor disputes.

* American Federationist, September 1915.

19. Facts

When S. G. wanted facts on tenement house production, he became a book agent and collected detailed statistics. Ever afterwards he advocated state bureaus of labor statistics to keep labor information currently available.

For the eight-hour movement, he instituted a system (1890) of annual report blanks for national and international unions—numerical strength, preparation for the movement, financial resources, etc. This constituted a kind of annual census that served many purposes. The categories under which data were supplied could be shifted as problems changed or developed.

Gompers pointed out in 1890 that the 1890 federal census law did not include provision for data on number unemployed and duration of unemployment and recommended an amendment to cover this omission. He himself maintained a crude index for a number of years which indicated trends.

In 1891 he submitted to the convention advocacy of a permanent census bureau and urged the convention to recommend the intimate association of twenty-eight existing state bureaus of labor statistics with a national census bureau under the Department of Labor.

Monthly he supplied the Federation's organizers with report blanks which were tabulated for publication in the American Federationist, the official magazine he edited. This United States and Canadian information from local labor unions supplied headquarters with useful information and served as an exchange suggestive for local unions in dealing with their problems.

His Federation factual services were limited but carefully chosen to serve functional needs. He might temporarily withhold information but he never "edited" after the political fashion of which George Orwell made us uncomfortably aware in "1984."

20. Private Property

Over and over Samuel Gompers declared: The trade union movement regards private property as a bulwark of individual freedom. The following summarizes his thinking:

The eternal problem with which the labor movement has to cope is control of property—to bring property into such relations to human life that it shall serve and not injure. The struggle has been long and hard but the day is past when the labor movement has to justify its right to be classified as a necessary agency with a function to perform in achieving greater freedom and justice. Its claim to acceptance as an instrumentality for achieving human progress is based upon the nature and the value of the service it renders. It was born out of efforts of workers to think out modern phases of that world-old universal problem—property.

Trade unions regard property and the laws of property as human institutions, intended for service in the development of individuality, giving each a feeling of security and assurance and independence, which mean freedom to direct and control his life. . .

It (the trade union movement) does not seek to overthrow private property. It regards private property as a necessary agency for securing opportunity for individual independence and resourcefulness, but it wishes to safeguard private property for use by preventing the perversion of property as an agency purely for exploitation and individual aggrandizement in order to establish an autocracy.*

In the post-war Reconstruction Program prepared under Mr. Gompers' supervision were included provisions to insure the inclusion of small farmers and tenants and small home owners in private ownership and control of agriculture and residential lands:

The private ownership of large tracts of usable land is not conducive to the best interests of a democratic people.

Legislation should be enacted placing a graduated tax upon all usable lands above the acreage which is cultivated by the owner. This should include provisions through which the tenant farmer, or

* American Federationist, November 1916.

133

others, may purchase land upon the lowest rate of interest and most favorable terms consistent with safety, and so safeguarded by governmental supervision and regulation as to give the fullest and freest opportunity for the development of land-owning agriculturists.

Special assistance should be given in the direction of allotments of land and the establishment of homes on the public domain.

Establishment of government experimental farms, measures for stock raising instruction, the irrigation of arid lands and reclamation of swamp and cut-over lands should be undertaken upon a larger scale under direction of the federal government.

Municipalities and states should be empowered to acquire lands for cultivation or the erection of residential buildings which they may use or dispose of under equitable terms.*

The inauguration of such a program would have increased enormously the distribution of private ownership and might have reduced attendant financial risks.

When Upton Sinclair proposed that the government take over and operate basic industries, Samuel Gompers replied in no uncertain terms:

Grown men who can read these propositions and not see that of necessity they blot out the present legal system, the established relations of the citizen to property, the independence of every individual, the liberty of movement, speech, press, assemblage—well, such men can believe black white, storm sunshine, war peace, cold heat, truth error, and insanity sanity. Men of such minds see society as through a mist, the creation of their own mental astigmatism.*

He concluded:

Without egotism, and I hope little if any vanity, I will say I came to the conclusion many years ago that it is our duty to live our lives as workers in the society in which we live and not to work for the downfall or the destruction or the overthrow of that society, but for its fuller development and evolution, that life may be the better worth the living; and if in the course of that effort some men are inconvenienced, then it is not to be ascribed to the failure of that natural and evolutionary movement, but rather to the credit of that movement, because it is the great conservator of peace and the public welfare.*

* Reconstruction Program, Convention Proceedings 1919, pp. 75–76.
* American Federationist, April 1914, "Upton Sinclair's Mental Marksmanship."
* Testimony, House Lobby Investigation Committee, Washington, D.C., December 1913.

Samuel Gompers realized that employers had a function separate and distinct from that of labor:

It is forgotten that the workman, too, has his "business" to manage, and that, to say the least, his part in production is as essential as that of capital.

When workmen insist upon certain terms, they are not seeking to control the employer's business, but to lay down the conditions of their own participation in that business.*

Of competition under a market economy he said:

Competition among mankind is to be encouraged or discouraged as it proves helpful or harmful to the race. By the tests of helpfulness or harmfulness it is legitimate or illegitimate. It is legitimate, and presumably will by necessity exist in all future society, of whatever form, when practiced under equal conditions of just opportunity to obtain the objects competed for among the human beings in any given group. It is illegitimate, in the present economic conditions of society, wherever men, deprived of their just opportunities for existence and self-development and the full products of their past labor, are obliged to compete through a forced sale of their labor power with other men similarly situated, to gain the necessaries of life.*

As to investment in securities and coupon clipping for income, he made this distinction:

Whether or not dividends should be paid as an incident to stock ownership regardless of the personal services performed, the activity or inactivity of the owner of the stock, depends altogether upon whether the investment is an honest one. An honest investment is an honest physical investment. . . . Very much of the opposition to the efforts of the working people to secure improved conditions has come from those who obtain what may be called an unearned share in distribution.*

* American Federationist, July 1902.
* American Federationist, November 1910.
* Statement, U.S. Commission on Industrial Relations, May 21–23, 1914, New York City.

21. Government

Samuel Gompers believed implicitly in government by law through a representative system. He believed men, not property, were the proper basis of representation in government. The provisions written into the American Constitution were to him a sacred trust to be evolved and extended but scrupulously maintained in essence. He approved extending suffrage to all adult persons so that the rights and interests of all groups would be proportionately considered and making more officials directly elective by citizens instead of appointive and indirectly responsible to citizens. He was for a time enthusiastic about the initiative and referendum but later modified his opinion. He related how a minority group formed a correspondence club by the initiative and referendum and took over control of the Cigarmakers International Union.*

The Cigarmakers experiment taught him how failure to hold regular and frequent conventions representative of all members limited the union's educational opportunities and facilitated formation of self-appointed groups to promote their special interests— "Government within government." Conspiratorial methods ending in minority rule always make for perversion or disintegration of an organization.

Gompers believed the checks and balances provided in our Federal constitution were the basic safeguard against despotism or arbitrary government:

For years the fathers wrestled with this great problem of self-government. The spirit that had called forth the sentiments and principles of the Declaration of Independence struggled and contested for a popular government in all that that expression implies.

* Convention Proceedings, 1915. President Gompers' statement on initiative and referendum.

The opposition, fearing to entrust the people with full sway, exerted their greatest efforts to limit the people's power. Yet all agreed upon one point, and that was, that the source of all power, of all new legislation, of every vital principle of law, should rest in the hands of the people through their representatives in Congress; aye, and by a two-thirds vote even over the veto of the President. In short, the Congress, composed of the House of Representatives and the Senate, was charged specifically under the basic laws contained in the Constitution, to make provision for revenues and expenditures, to establish a fiscal system, and above and beyond all to form a code of law, in respect to which the executive and judicial branches of the Government were and are required to yield obedience, these branches on this point being not coordinate, but subordinate. For example, the executive was granted no authority to create law; the law was to be made solely and distinctly by the people's representatives in Congress, and then it was designed that the judicial department should administer the law as it found it, and the executive should execute the law as it was clearly written and interpreted.*

He pointed out evils from excessive law making:

... There is a steadily growing disposition to shift responsibility for personal progress and welfare to outside agencies.

What can be the result of this tendency but the softening of the moral fibre of the people? When there is unwillingness to accept responsibility for one's life and for making the most of it there is a loss of strong, red-blooded, rugged independence and will power to grapple with the wrong of the world and to establish justice through the volition of those concerned.

Many of the things for which many are so deludedly demanding legislative regulation should and must be worked out by those concerned. Initiative, aggressive conviction, enlightened self-interest, are the characteristics that must be dominant among the people if the nation is to make substantial progress toward better living and higher ideals. Legislation cannot secure those characteristics but it can facilitate or impede them. Laws can not create and superimpose the ideals sought, they can only free people from the shackles and give them a chance to work out their own salvation.

Many conscientious and zealous persons think that every evil, every mistake, every unwise practice, can be straightway corrected by law.

There is among some critics of prevailing conditions a belief

---

* President's report, Convention Proceedings, 1910.

that legislation is a short-cut to securing any desired reform—merely enact a law and the thing is done.

Now enacting a law and securing the realization of the purpose the law is aimed to secure are two vastly different matters. . . .

A law that really is a law, is a result of public thought and conviction and not a power to create thought or conviction. The enforcement of the law follows naturally because the people will it. To enact a law with the hope and for the purpose of educating the people is to proceed by indirection and to waste energy. It is better to begin work for securing ideals by directing activity first for fundamentals. Frequently, when the people concerned become mindful and eager for what will promote their own welfare, they find that they are much more able to secure what will benefit and adapt their methods to changing circumstances than is any law or the administration of that law.*

His final warning:

We must not as a nation allow ourselves to drift upon a policy that eats at and will surely undermine the very foundations of personal freedom.

Labor seeks legislation from the hands of government for such purposes only as the individuals or groups of workers can not effect for themselves, and for the freedom and the right to exercise their normal activities in the industrial and social struggle for the protection and promotion of their rights and interests and for the accomplishment of their highest and best ideals.*

Gompers obviously believed rights and freedom could be maintained when individuals and groups learned that society is governed by many public and private codes and controls and that they must use discrimination in channelling problems to the control that can assure competence and authority—social, economic or political—and then carefully and regularly check up on administration whether public or private. He frequently quoted Junius as saying, "Eternal vigilance is the price of liberty."

He believed that provisions making property ownership a requirement for voting should be abolished leaving only personal requirements. He maintained that when the government assumed functions formerly performed by private organizations such organizations should appoint com-

* American Federationist, February 1915.
* American Federationist, February 1915.

petent advisers to aid the administrative agency in carrying out duties.

Labor has a right to representation on all agencies that control or determine public policies or matters of general concern. This assertion of rights has come with the startling challenge of a new demand. Democratic organization of society is a commonplace term that has not the force of full reality in the affairs of life and work. . . .

The basis for representation and participation in the affairs of organized society is man not property. The purpose of social organization is the furtherance of human rights, interests, justice and liberty—it seeks to achieve a beautiful ideal—fullness of life and opportunity for all. The workers, the masses of the people therefore have a right to participate and will insist upon this participation in the determination and control of all that concerns their lives and the lives of the generations yet to come.*

Foreign Policy

Like every person whose life has been filled with conflicts and battles for justice, Samuel Gompers had real appreciation of peace. Like most workers with a European inheritance of reactions, he was at first automatically a pacifist and anti-militarist. He moved rather slowly in modifying proposals as did many other pacifists—from anti-militarism, opposition to large standing armies and large navies, to advocacy of international arbitration, international court, limitation of armament, etc.

In 1898 he summarized traditional American foreign policy thus:

America, and particularly American institutions, are not only worthy of our love and veneration because they give us greater freedom than those of any other nation, but the institutions of the United States represent a principle—the great principle of self-government of the people, for the people, by the people—self-restraint as well as great power. This principle we shall only prove ourselves worthy of representing, and holding forth as an inspiration for the peoples of other nations to emulate and seek to establish by manifesting restraint upon ourselves or upon those who would thrust us out of our physical, moral, progressive and powerful sphere into the vortex of imperialism, with all the evils which that term implies—

* Report prepared by President Gompers for Executive Council, 1916 Convention Proceedings.

militarism, despotism, and venality on the one hand; slavery, misery and despair on the other.

The flag of our Republic should float over a free people, and must never form a cloak to hide slavery, barbarism, despotism or tyranny.*

In addition he reported to the 1898 A. F. of L. Convention on the struggle for self-government of the islands of the old Spanish Empire on our frontiers:

From the ranks of labor came the quarter of a million men who volunteered to sacrifice their lives upon the altar of their country in so great a cause. Who, then, but the representatives of labor have the better right to consider the very grave questions which have resulted from our war with Spain? . . .

Out of the war have grown questions of the most serious moment to our people generally and of direct interest to the wage-earners particularly.

Is it not strange, that, after entering upon a war with Spain to obtain the freedom and independence of Cuba, now that victory has been achieved, the question of Cuban independence is often scouted? Our people were ardent and honest in advocacy of Cuban freedom, and are impatient at any attempt to juggle with the question. When the people of Cuba desire annexation to our country it is time to discuss the subject; and in the meantime the fruits of the victory for which they have striven so long and so valiantly, and for which we went to war to aid them to achieve, must not be ruthlessly taken from them. . .

The A. F. of L. in unmistakable tones opposed the annexation of Hawaii . . .

He then reviewed factual developments from the war:

Puerto Rico, invaded as a war measure, has been conquered and taken as a possession.

At Manila, of the Philippine Islands, where the Spanish fleet was annihilated. . . We are confronted with the awful spectacle of our republic, founded, and for a century and a quarter successfully existing, upon the basis of the principle that governments derive their just powers from the consent of the governed; our great republic of America, face to face with the insurgents of Manila, seeking by the force of arms to compel their submission; recognizing that their

* President's Report, Convention Proceedings, 1898.

cause would be a forlorn hope against the mighty power of our arms, sullenly yielding to superior force. . .

We cannot annex the Philippines without a large increase in our standing army. A large standing army is repugnant to republican institutions and a menace to the liberty of our own people.

If we annex the Philippines, we shall have to conquer the Filipinos by force of arms, and thereby deny to them what we claim for ourselves—the right of self-government.

We shall surrender the present safe and independent position by which we are guaranteed the tranquillity and the fruits of peace, and force ourselves into European and Asiatic entanglements implying war and the preparation for war. We shall become a militant instead of a peace-loving nation. We shall seek to conquer by the force of arms instead of by our own industry, commerce and superior mentality and civilization. We shall be compelled to open the gates and admit the Chinese Malays and slave laborers who may come from "our new possessions," since the constitution of the United States forbids the interdiction of the free entry of men and their products between our states and our territories. . . .

The attempt to divert the attention of our people from the ills from which we suffer at home to foreign questions will fail. The principles of liberty and justice have been imbibed by our people too many years to permit them to be cheated out of their birthright. The institutions of our republic have taken root too deeply in the minds and hearts of our people to permit us to become a nation of conquerors, or to dominate by force of arms, a people struggling for liberty and independence.*

Mr. Gompers repeatedly referred to the "imperialists" and "expansionists" who urged ratification of the Spanish treaty by which the United States took possession of Spain's island empire but did not identify them. He reported to the 1899 convention:

A marked change within the recent past has overcome the policy and trend of our country in its international relations. A humane war, undertaken for the independence of Cuba from Spanish domination and misrule and the circumstances in connection therewith, has been taken advantage of to ruthlessly trample under foot every principle upon which our Republic was founded; every tradition which has made its name sacred to patriots, thinkers, and humanitarians, and every policy which has endeared the names of the statesmen, heroes, and emancipators, have been flagrantly flung to the winds.

* President's report, Convention Proceedings, 1898.

Hawaii is annexed in spite of the protests of her people. Slave-like conditions of labor obtain there.*

He charged that "coercion and threats of the most far reaching character were employed to change the votes of some Senators from the opposition to, to approval of, the treaty."

He in the above quotation and at other times referred to manipulation of foreign war and crises as one of the oldest tricks of diplomacy to distract domestic attention from problems at home.

Between 1899 and the beginning of World War I a great change came in Mr. Gompers' statements on foreign policy which he characterized as abandonment of pacifism. Would he have altered his counsel if he could have seen the verification of his prophecy of '99 through the developments of World War I and its consequences resulting in World War II and cold war, our government blinded in the fog of international power policies, when moral principles and standards on which our Republic was founded are no longer the compass, and when at least ten percent of national product is absorbed by the military, and the United States maintains nearly a thousand armed establishments encircling the globe though it is restrained from battle conflict by the destructiveness of the atomic bombs it has brought to mass production output?

One wonders whether today Gompers would find that the same agents who laid the foundations of our territorial empire are now directing our global commercial empire, using the same threats and coercion to assure their needed "defense budgets" so that a few corporations use large amounts of national wealth for private gain. Defense appropriations constituting eighty percent of the federal budget are justified by fear and distrust which such agents themselves seem to manipulate.

Just before World War I he prepared a speech to be made in Plattsburg in commemoration of the decisive battle of our last war with Great Britain and the beginning of one hundred years of peace. After the day the Kaiser's divisions began to march in World War I, he said:

* President's Report, Convention Proceedings, 1899, p. 16.

Government must be founded upon justice and morality. In ancient societies individuals undertook to enforce their own claims to justice and standards of morality. Each had the right to private warfare. With the development of society the duty of maintaining justice and peace was delegated to governmental agencies. The maintenance of justice and peace between nations is now emerging from the same chaotic conditions which formerly characterized the relations between individuals. There are evidences which intimate that intelligence will emerge out of this chaos—international solidarity of labor, international law, treaties of peace and commerce, arbitration treaties, The Hague Tribunal. With these accumulating institutions to bind the nations together, there is developing a code of international morality and a habit of mind necessary to enforce standards of international morality upon all.*

"Government must be founded upon justice and morality"—he declared and also indicated that peace can be facilitated by conscious sustained efforts to develop the agencies and the methods to attain it:

Just as the governing aristocracies have studied efficiency in attaining their purposes and in controlling the affairs of the country, so the people must perfect the agents and the methods of democracy. They must take in their own hands the ordering of their own lives and interests and insist that governments shall manage these things with justice and peace.

The maintenance of justice and peace is worthy of all the expenditure and thought and effort and skill that have been given to the arts of war. Furthermore these ends can not be attained without such expenditure. The peace of the world will be determined by the decision of the nations.*

Supported by these high hopes, he faced the world war situation quite ready for national preparedness as a basic policy and to abandon neutrality. He was ready to assume a responsible office in readying the country for defense of rights and justice which he realized must be the basis of world peace. He also opposed efforts to negotiate peace without victory.

From the first he opposed recognition of the counter-revolution of the Bolshevists in Russia. In 1919 he pointed to the heart of the evil:

* Address at Plattsburg, N.Y., September 7, 1914.
* Address at Plattsburg, N.Y., September 7, 1914. American Federationist, October 1914.

Russia stands before our gaze like a flaming torch of warning. A thing called Bolshevism has reared its ugly head in that sad and sorry land. Bolshevism is a theory, the chief tenet of which is the "dictatorship of the proletariat". Leaving out of consideration for the moment the story of murder and devastation that has marched with this theory into practice, we must set down the theory itself as abhorrent to a world that loves democracy. We shall progress by the use of the machinery of democracy, or we shall not progress. There is no group of men on earth fit to dictate to the rest of the world. It is this central idea of Bolshevism that makes the whole of it outcast in the minds of sane men. It is this focusing point of it all that makes it an enemy to our civilization.

This idea—the central theory of Bolshevism—is not in the minds of the people of Russia.*

And yet he frequently warned against what he called "invisible government" operating through our representative system to steal control away from the people who thought they were controlling through their votes and party affiliation:

These are but a few of the evidences of the powerful and subtle conspiracy between organized capital and the governmental agents of the State indicating the existence of the "invisible government" that steals from the workers the liberty they think and are told they have.*

S. G. wrote into the annual Executive Council Report for 1921 an endorsement of refusal to recognize the Soviet counter-revolutionary government imposed upon the Russian people without their consent:

The American Federation of Labor is not justified in taking any action which could be construed as an assistance to, approval of, the soviet government of Russia so long as that government is based upon authority which has not been vested in it by a popular representative national assemblage of the Russian people or so long as it endeavors to create revolutions in the established civilized nations of the world; or so long as it advocates and applies the militarization of labor and prevents the organizing and functioning of trade unions and the maintenance of a free press and free public assemblage.*

* From "The Battle Line of Labor," McClure's Magazine, May 1919.
* American Federationist, 1913, page 829.
* Report prepared for Executive Council, 1921 Convention Proceedings.

22. World War I

S. G. seemed no more prepared for the Kaiser's marching order to his troops than the majority of citizens of this country. He was a member of a number of pacifist organizations and had denounced militarism, compulsory military training and service in vehement terms. His speeches and the record of his activities for peace had been readied for publication as World War I disrupted peace. This manuscript included the speech for the meeting in Plattsburg, New York, in celebration of the hundredth anniversary of the decisive battle of Plattsburg which inaugurated a century of peace between the United States and Great Britain, a meeting that coincided with the beginning of fighting in Europe. He hastened to withdraw his peace manuscript from the Carnegie Foundation. He seemed much disturbed either by his intuition that world war was imminent or perhaps advance information reached him. He had hoped that international ties between unions would remain a restraining force between peoples and private groups for peace even though governments might declare war. As he watched this vision dissolve, he seemed to clear his mind for orienting himself in the new world situation. When he had accumulated basic information on changed problems and decided how to deal with them, he made an organizing and speaking tour through Canada. He came back overflowing with their spirit of devotion to England as the mother of parliamentary government and personal freedom. The basic theme of his public speaking was:

Patriotism is a strong compelling force—a primal instinct in the individual.*

Then he fervently quoted Rudyard Kipling:

* Samuel Gompers, Harpers' Weekly, August 7, 1915.

"Should the lights of freedom go out in England they go out all over the world."

He was quite oblivious to Great Britain's invasion of our freedom on the high seas but recounted vividly damages to our shipping and losses of American lives by German submarines. He seemed personally committed to aid Great Britain and convinced that that course would provide security for democracy. He had several favorite poems expressing patriotic emotion which he quoted or read to visitors who came to consult with him. A most fervidly patriotic poem written by a Washington barber he would read—or ask the barber poet to read—in his deep orotone. He favored a French engineer with this special tonic. The engineer, a member of the French Military Commission charting its defense production, listened quietly, but in obvious self-restraint.

S. G. expressed his sense of responsibility as follows:

> The people who are willing to maintain their rights and to defend their freedom are worthy of those privileges. Rights carry with them obligation—duty. It is the duty of those who live under free institutions at least to maintain them unimpaired.*

S. G. as he said often frankly of himself was a partisan—never a neutral. He was devoted to the country of his birth and the country of his choice and understood the interconnection of their institutions,—England the mother of parliamentary institutions and the United States which adapted the representative principle to pioneer needs. He saw the mistakes and shortcomings of Germany, but for the countries that had been home he reserved the spirit voiced by Browning's Rabbi Ben Ezra—

"Not what I am but what I would be
That am I worth to God."

Mr. Gompers early sensed that the polyglot nature of our nation was a potential hazard in a war involving such large world areas. Knowing the make-up of our national labor force and the strength of love of former fatherland latent in even second generation immigrants, he realized that immediate and organized efforts were needed to achieve unity for the cause and policy our country might follow. He

---

* Address, National Civic Federation, January 18, 1916.

travelled systematically through strategic areas talking to key individuals and rousing them as citizens as well as trade unionists to awareness of different dangers and responsibility under war conditions. Such groups were the Germans, other hyphenated Americans, the Irish to whom free Ireland was paramount, the Socialists, etc. Many immigrants settled in neighborhoods dominated by fellow countrymen and organized in national groups, still speaking their home country language, maintaining many old country customs, and were served by foreign language publications. They sometimes organized churches and schools to maintain former national languages and customs. Workers, especially Germans and Italians, formed unions of their former countrymen in which German or Italian was the language for conducting business.

There were among these immigrant groups designated as hyphenated, many who were loyal members of trade unions and who had contributed substantially to their growth and strength here. The Irish have a genius for politics and were active in political parties as well as in trade unions where they as gallant leaders added fire and endurance. Their religious grounding in personal dignity and freedom facilitated and strengthened the incorporation of these principles in trade unionism. Italians also organized and led their own kinsmen into organizations through which the New World functions. Germans and others of Teutonic stock had been resourceful and developed competence in community and group undertakings. The very fact that these and others had initiative and influence made them targets for the war propaganda of their former countries as well as useful to their adopted country. Because of what they were and could do, Mr. Gompers was anxious they should understand what was happening and how they could be of service. Obviously these foreign language communities could be used for the United States or against the United States. S. G. wanted to make sure these wage-earners were not trapped into indiscretions by failure to understand the difference between peace and war conditions. Especially he warned Irish trade unionists whose devoted zeal to free Ireland at that time might easily bring trouble to them and our country. He wanted to make sure they understood that the tolerances which were the pride of peace would not obtain during war.

Hyphenated groups were served by a number of foreign business agencies such as banks and insurance companies which gathered information useful for their home industries in war as well as in peace. He accumulated wide information through such channels at the same time he was strengthening the trade union movement for a new test and strain and educating leaders for a new field of responsibility and service. He kept close watch over organizations with international affiliations likely to favor pacifist or peace propaganda such as the socialists and communists and vigilantly safeguarded key unions such as longshoremen and other transportation and communication workers. He counseled with his trade union card group in Congress so that they might be wary of peace propaganda and disguised pro-Kaiser policies.

Soon after Great Britain declared war on Germany two labor men were sent over to the United States, apparently by the British Defense Administration, one of whom was a special friend of Samuel Gompers. He advised with them. No official record or contact was established. They were the forerunners of a goodly procession from many countries that continued throughout the war. He had trusted emissaries for various purposes and no one in his confidence knew them all or the details of various lines of effort. He was exuberant and stimulated by the scope and the importance of his responsibilities which his representative office brought him and worked tirelessly for the cause to which he dedicated himself. He felt his responsibility as leader of a large cross-section of American citizens and prepared himself to rouse them to the meaning of developments and their corresponding duties.

When Congress enacted legislation authorizing a Council of National Defense supplemented by an Advisory Commission of private citizens, S. G. was appointed to the Commission. He obtained the approval of the Executive Council of the American Federation of Labor before accepting the honor as well as the responsibility for service.

Mr. Gompers' first glimpse of what war involved industrywise came through the survey of industries convertible to war production which Howard Coffin, another member of the Advisory Commission, made before our government declared war. He seemed fascinated by this over-all inventory of capacity, resources and potential technical development.

War Labor Problems

A month previous to a declaration of war by Congress, Mr. Gompers had called an emergency conference of national labor executives who adopted a declaration of support for this Republic in peace or in war—a heartening declaration for the nation and the President of the Republic. Then began officially his task of mobilizing American Labor in support of the American Republic. To aid him in his work of the Advisory Commission, he invited the executives of all national and international unions, the railway brotherhoods and a number of employers and representatives of the public to advise and work with him. It was an unusual group that seemed eager to meet and work jointly with representatives of other groups. The Committee had one full-dress meeting to which a commission of British labor representatives were invited to report principles and plans for war labor administration under which they were operating.

Mr. Gompers then appointed committees constituted similarly to his master committee. The functions and set-up of these committees provided a chart for war labor administration later followed by the Department of Labor when its Secretary became the war labor administrator. One notable undertaking resulted in war insurance for sailors and soldiers. The work of these committees developed characteristic pioneer adaptations of civilian procedures with use of functioning institutions which were carried over to governmental plans when the war administration legislation was enacted. The use of voluntary economic agencies and the cooperation of voluntary organizations forestalled over-expansion of government machinery and staff, which in turn minimized raiding of public funds which has developed so extravagantly during the second world war and the present "cold war." With S. G. voluntarism was part of the very fibre of his personality. He took great personal pride in helping to extend contractual principles to work relations in war production even though it involved foregoing the union shop which the government thought it could not legally negotiate.

After war was declared against Germany and her allies, action had to come quickly on war provisions with high priority such as mobilization of fighting personnel and the building of cantonments, ships, the manufacture of uniforms and conversion of factories for war products. Coordination of planning and policies was through the Council of National Defense.

He emphasized the importance of civilian war effort and the need to maintain civilian institutions:

We should bear in mind this further fact, that all of the fighting men who could answer to the call to arms, whether two millions or five millions or more, would have been of no avail whatsoever if it had not been for the civilian fighting man in factory, workshop and shipyard. It is the heroism of industry, it is the heroism of a consciousness that very few people outside the ranks of labor can understand or appreciate.*

S. G. was in a position to represent Labor in the development of policies and to insist upon labor representation at various administrative levels. Contracts had to be let and long range plans developed to insure rapid and uninterrupted production. Practical, experienced men in key positions expanded and used existing private organizations to meet emergency needs. The Secretary of War, Newton D. Baker, asked a resourceful young attorney to take over initial responsibility for him. Louis B. Wehle, a lawyer with experience in the railway industry, with a mind uncluttered by preconceptions, presented a daring simple plan to the Secretary and S. G.—a business contract between government and labor. To escape delays, Baker and S. G. assumed responsibility and signed the following contract:

June 19, 1917.

For the adjustment and control of wages, hours and conditions of labor in the construction of cantonments, there shall be created an adjustment commission of three persons, appointed by the Secretary of

* Address, Labor Victory Meeting, New York City, December 1, 1918.

War: one to represent the Army, one the public and one labor; the last to be nominated by Samuel Gompers, member of the Advisory Commission of the Council of National Defense, and President of the American Federation of Labor.

As basic standards with reference to each cantonment, such commission shall use the union scales of wages, hours and conditions in force on June 1, 1917, in the locality where such cantonment is situated. Consideration shall be given to special circumstances, if any, arising after said date which may require particular advances in wages or changes in other standards. Adjustment of wages, hours, or conditions made by such board are to be treated as binding by all parties.*

Newton D. Baker
Sam'l Gompers

Secretary of the Navy Daniels undersigned the agreement as applying to Navy construction work. All knew they might be charged with exceeding their legal authority but mindful of desperate national need they took action to speed an army in the field.

Mr. Gompers voiced the controlling urge which enabled them to get cooperation:

One of the strongest impulses in man is patriotism. This instinct was ignored by internationalism. Yet it is the instinct that has ever inspired men to make great and heroic sacrifices—to give up interests, possessions, dear ones, and even life itself. Patriotism lifts men above the level of expediency, safety, and profits. War is awful but patriotism will dare even war. The man who has thought only for his personal safety and welfare may be useful but he is not inspiring. But the man or the woman who gives ungrudgingly, with glorious disregard of self, is an inspiration that brings us close to the beauty and the purpose of life, and makes luminous the ideal—"He lives most who gives most."*

Then Gompers and Wehle undertook the job of getting employers and workers to start operations under this contract even before the necessary enabling legislation and funds were available. Wehle appealed to the patriotism of employers and Gompers to the patriotism of union executives. A number of contracts between governmental agencies

* The full story of this and other contracts is reported by Louis B. Wehle in his book, "Hidden Threads of History," as well as in the reports of S. G. prepared for A. F. of L. Conventions 1917, 1918 and 1919.

* American Federationist, November 1914.

and the responsible unions and employers willing to take the risk, organized discipline for various war undertakings.

The contract covering cantonments was later extended to all war construction for the War and Navy Departments and for the Emergency Fleet Corporation. Similar agreements were later developed for war munitions by the responsible agencies and trade unions of workers employed in such production, with a national War Labor Board to deal with controversies. In dealing with his war labor problems, Mr. Gompers applied American trade union principles and precepts, so that the transition to war production mobilization was made with as little confusion and difficulty as possible. Unions supplied the necessary workers and helped train and adjust workers for war work, and were strengthened by opportunities for more varied services. Unions and industries supplied existing disciplined agencies through which the government could channel orders without dislocating the controls and economic order of private organizations. There was the minimum of danger to responsible self-government inherent in temporary administrative agencies.

NATIONAL MORALE

Mr. Gompers, whose keen insight was in part based on the fact he was an immigrant and had personally experienced other than United States conditions, designated as the two great divisive forces in the country, the Socialist Party and the foreign language press which was controlled mainly from New York. The National Committee on Public Information directed by George Creel had been organized to controvert subversive propaganda among various groups. S. G. interested the agency in these two problems.

Because the Socialists with their emphasis on international principles and action were a vulnerable element in national unity, Mr. Gompers was instrumental in having a number of the more constructive leaders who had withdrawn from the Socialist Party interviewed on an avowal of support for the nation. These persons expressed willingness to take leadership for the emergency and to cooperate with trade union leaders for that purpose. The People's

Council, an agency for promoting thinking and action favorable to Germany, had planned a national conference in St. Paul. This Council had a Workingmen's Division which was active in war industries.

Mr. Gompers planned a trade unionist-socialist conference for the same time and place as the meeting of the People's Council. He personally invited trade unionists as individuals—probably the only procedure to which they would respond. St. Paul, which had had considerable trouble with left wing activity among its foreign born groups, refused a permit for the People's Council meeting. Regretful to lose his dramatic background, Mr. Gompers went ahead with his meeting. It was a curious mixture of restrained socialist oratory and trade unionist practical talk which resulted in a workable truce for co-existence and a joint statement putting national allegiance before international obligations for war guidance of all socialists and trade unionists.

As a result of the St. Paul conference, the American Alliance for Labor and Democracy was formed. It was very influential in combatting "peace" propaganda and various other efforts to weaken support for the Administration program. This organization was directed out of the Federation offices. Prominent Socialists were thus diverted from international control and given responsibility by our Government.

As his knowledge of East Side New York and foreign-born groups was wider than that of most people, he also took the iniative in dealing with the foreign press problem. He called conferences of editors of foreign language papers in New York and set up channels in the American Federation of Labor office for official information to be made available to them to counteract German propaganda disseminated through the "People's Council" which organized Workingmen's Councils to service trade unionists and socialists with their propaganda.

Mr. Gompers was also much concerned lest the minority group to which he belonged by birth should create ill will against itself by unnecessarily evidencing dissension with Administration undertakings. When he went to New

York to confer with a powerful Jewish leader, he asked Secretary Morrison to accompany him as there were a number of other war labor problems to be dealt with. Just outside the office door of this Jewish leader, Samuel Gompers paused, reached in his pocket and pulled out a black skull cap. When he put this on, his whole personality seemed to change as he entered the room and began conference with other cap-wearing men seated around the table. The United Hebrew Trades was one of the agencies whose cooperation could help keep foreign-language publications loyal to the Government.

In this period practically all trade unions ceased using foreign language as their official medium for meetings and publications and established the general practice of one language for all collective business—in itself a powerful force in Americanization of foreign-born and hyphenated citizenry.

INTERNATIONAL SERVICE

When he had tidied up the main home defense problems, Mr. Gompers turned to international aspects. The many foreign delegations had noted appreciatively how tightly the workers of this country were united in support of winning the war. Their own labor forces had not been so effectively coordinated in the war administration by a leader operating as member of the government war team and were constrained by distrust engendered by centuries of empire-building governments busy during war as well as peace. Some socialists and European trade unionists felt that efforts for peace were never out of order and began to promote peace movements to bring pressure on their governments to save lives and reduce post war problems. Mr. Gompers expressed his attitude toward peace and these developments thus:

The American labor movement never advocated peace at any price. It never encouraged nor gave support to any movement of peace at any price. While it recognizes that peace is essential for normal, progressive development, it steadfastly refused to advocate peace at the sacrifice of the ideals of freedom and justice.*

* "Our Shield Against Bolshevism," McClure's Magazine, April 1919.

They all learned again that governments became absolute when at war and that national ties in war time have priority over those uniting workers to international organizations or groups. Mr. Gompers seemed to have no doubt that the best interests of free nations lay in alliance of the United States with Great Britain and France and used all of his powers of persuasion to convince others to that belief. His fervor and enthusiasm made him an invaluable asset for that cause.

The Internationale was active directly through its national socialist branches and indirectly through socialists members of trade unions. The Internationale planned a conference to be held in Stockholm to consider peace terms and thereby avert further loss of lives. It invited the socialists and trade unionists of all countries to attend. Mr. Gompers pointed out that international socialism as well as the International Secretariat (trade unionists) had their international headquarters in Germany and were largely under German control at the outbreak of the war and that German participation in undertakings would be permitted only if the German government thought to gain advantage. Therefore he held it was unwise to attempt to confer on plans or policies while Germany was in a strong position. Even after the International Secretariat headquarters was moved to Amsterdam it could not function normally. Gompers had information that a number of German trade unionists were spending much time in Switzerland and in that way keeping in touch with trade unionists and socialists who passed through and doing a bit of brain washing. He was fearful of the effect on labor morale of conferences such as were planned for Stockholm and Berne and felt confident he could counterbalance these undertakings by uniting trade unionists of Europe in support of the war as well as convince European statesmen they must really consult with their labor leaders to hold their cooperation and support.

He was from the first anxious to develop agreement on conservative post-war policies along constructive lines and realized that unless initiative and specific suggestions came from trade unionists the socialist-totalitarians would take the initiative.

S. G. charged that Reich funds financed the "peace" propaganda emanating from Switzerland and other neutral countries. S. G. declined all invitations to Socialist conferences. But when an invitation came from Arthur Henderson on behalf of the National Executive of the British Labor Party, he took the invitation up with his Executive Council who directed him to state the position of United States labor: they would not meet with representatives of a nation at war with us. Later, when he had decided it timely to make a tour of the allied countries, he asked that an Inter-Allied Labor Conference be arranged to be held in London. S. G. thought Arthur Henderson intended to turn the labor meeting into a socialist undertaking and hoped to scotch that by attacking the fallacies and shortcomings of socialism, declaring it destroyed personal initiative and wiped out national pride. Gompers himself had concluded patriotism was a primal instinct which should wisely be made to aid at the international level also.

By precise, well-planned team work S. G. and his team controlled the declarations emanating from the Conference. They recalled attention of all allied governments to the basic importance of coordinating Labor's activities for the war effort and thereby strengthening national unity and morale. They also reminded workers their most effective medium for cooperating was their organized economic power—trade unions.

During World War I, S. G. found he must continue his opposition to socialism and broadened the scope of his charges against it. As he repeatedly declared, the theory of socialism-communism was evolved in Germany by Karl Marx and his disciples and the party operated as a German agency. This party organized national branches in other countries and coordinated their policies. As he affirmed, the American Socialist party consisted of Socialists of several nationalities chiefly German and some Americans. He affirmed there had been an understanding between the party and the Imperial German Government by which the Socialists voted solidly for military appropriations for the German

war-machine and helped spread propaganda that the German army would be used to maintain the peace of the world.

The Reich enacted health insurance legislation which
gave it a tool for regimenting labor, tolerated socialism
which taught "everything must be done by the Government."
Socialists, he declared, in all countries tried to capture all
kinds of labor meetings to substitute their doctrine for
trade unionism. The Reich planned to dominate the world,
he charged in Europe and in meetings he addressed in
Canada and the United States.*

In a speech to the Canadian House of Commons, he
charged:

There is no question but what there was an understanding between the socialist political leaders of Germany and the German
Imperialist Government to carry out its policies. The socialists in the
German Reichstag voted solidly for the military credits of that Government. The socialists of Germany began the propaganda years and
years ago to instil into the minds of the peoples of other countries
that which was in accord with their Emperor's declaration that he
was a war lord, but he proposed to use the great army of Germany to
maintain the peace of the world; and the propaganda of the German
socialists was to hypnotize the people of all the other countries into
believing that there was no need on their part, on our part, to prepare against any hostile demonstration on the part of the German
army.

I never was fooled by the sophistry and pretences of the socialists.
As a matter of fact, there is not in England, France nor America a
socialist party of those countries. In America we have a German
branch of the German socialist party. The Socialist Party of the
United States is made up of different nationalities and some Americans.*

European governments realized the need of keeping
the American economy at top level capacity to equip armed
forces in minimum time as well as to strengthen their own
efforts, and helped to make Mr. Gompers' tour of countries

* Address in the Armories, Toronto, Canada, November 28, 1917; Convention National Lecturers Association, Washington, D.C., April 11, 1918;
public meeting, Rome, Italy, October 8, 1918; Parliament, Ottawa, Canada,
April 27, 1918.
* House of Commons, Ottawa, April 27, 1918.

and battlefronts an ovation and notable success. He visited capitals, addressed parliaments, all appropriate civilian groups and then troops on battle-fronts. His whole personality was keyed for the effort and he thoroughly appreciated the honors and adulation bestowed on him. His triumphant tour was sharply and dramatically ended by the news of the death of his only living daughter.

The tour was a record achievement for trade unionism and the power of a dedicated union representative.

23. Post War

INTERNATIONAL LABOR GLOBAL

Mr. Gompers early began planning policies and agencies to maintain peace after the fighting war should end.

When the political genius of the nations provides representative machinery for dealing with international relations, diplomacy will catch step with democratic ideals of freedom and justice. But any plan which purposes merely to deny nations the right to use force will fail. Force can not be eliminated, but it should be under the control of intelligent, responsible, democratically controlled agents of justice. Organized responsible force will make treaties something more than scraps of paper. International peace will follow international justice —not disarmament and proscription of war . . . However, let no one be deluded into thinking that international political organization will supplant the national state. The present war has proved that one of the strongest emotions in men is patriotism. Patriotism is a strong compelling force—a primal instinct in the individual. It was stronger than the fundamental tenet of socialism, stronger than ideals of international peace, stronger than religion, stronger than love of life and family.[*]

In the first Federation Convention following the opening of hostilities in Europe, he introduced a resolution which proposed the holding of a world trade union conference simultaneously with the peace congress that would follow the war and in the same city. In that way Labor would have current opportunity to oppose or approve plans in the making and perhaps prevent or counsel on undertakings affecting the welfare of wage-earners of all nations. The purpose he advocated was effectuated in a different way from what he had foreseen.

President Wilson appointed S. G. and Edward N. Hurley[*] to serve on the International Labor Commission

[*] Harper's Weekly, August 7, 1915.
[*] Later replaced by Henry M. Robinson.

159

which drafted the labor provisions of the Versailles Peace Treaty—Part XIII. As chairman of that Commission S. G. was advised by the American trade unionists whom the Executive Council of the Federation selected to accompany him to Europe. The Commission drafted Part XIII of the Versailles Treaty. He worked hard to provide labor and industry with constructive functions in the International Labor Organization and to forestall preoccupation with legislation and to restrict consideration of union problems so as not to interfere in the field best governed through collective bargaining and contract between representatives of those directly concerned. As a fundamental and overriding principle he won agreement to include the following: "The labor of a human being is not a commodity or article of commerce."

The Commission provided for a Labor Charter and a governmental agency so effective that it was one of the few agencies of the League of Nations to function through and survive World War II and the only one incorporated in the United Nations when it replaced the League of Nations. The United States Congress failed to ratify the Versailles Treaty so American labor did not affiliate to the I.L.O. in S. G.'s lifetime.

He with other representatives of the American Federation of Labor took part in the conference which reorganized the International Secretariat under the new name: International Federation of Trade Unions. There he unfortunately became involved in a controversy with Karl Legien. Legien was no radical although a Socialist. He was first of all a German citizen and next a trade unionist. When the declaration of war between Germany and the United States was nearly consummated, S. G. had cabled Karl Legien asking him to prevail upon the German government to avert a break with the United States. Legien had replied that action on his part was hopeless unless the United States prevailed on Britain to end the blockade which was starving the German nation and appealed to American Labor not to become cat's paws of war profiteers by sailing in war zones. Although this interchange of messages had something of the aspect of shadow-boxing to onlookers, it seemed to have real meaning to the two men concerned. If these two powerful trade union leaders when they met in Amsterdam after the war could have laid aside all prejudices and talked together without language difficulties, they could have controlled trends which later gave advantages to advocates of totalitarian methods and purposes. As it was, the Federation was not protected against unfair allocating of costs in the new International constitution or against automatic use of their representatives' signatures to official documents embodying socialist ideals and policies, and therefore refused to affiliate.

S. G. saw quite clearly that we should make international peace a positive goal with organized agencies and systematic work to achieve and maintain it through justice in daily life and work:

> Twentieth century nations must adopt as a principle of government that peace is a basis of all civilization. Peace is not a by-product of other conditions, but it is a condition that can be secured by agents and institutions designed to maintain it. Peace is the fundamental necessity for all government and progress—industrial, intellectual, social and humanitarian. Without peace all these are as nothing. One of the main purposes of governments then must be the maintenance of international peace.*

He also felt that:

> International peace will result only from international agencies for establishing justice, possessing power to enforce its decisions. Peace at any cost is advocated by only sentimentalists and neurotic dreamers. The best guarantee of peace to any self-respecting independent nation is the power of self-protection.*

WESTERN HEMISPHERE—INTERNATIONAL

However S. G. had some compensation in seeing the principles of economic trade unionism find their way into Mexico and other Latin-American countries. He had for many years kept in touch with Mexican workers who sought refuge in the United States.

The revolution of 1916 which established constitutional government based on principles of representation and rights of citizens afforded opportunity for S. G. to counsel

---

* Address, Plattsburg, New York, September 7, 1914.
* Harper's Weekly, August 7, 1915.

with Mexican workers on the organization of a trade union movement to promote their economic welfare and bargain for higher wages and shorter hours as well as for real participation in decisions on national policies. S. G. was able to intervene for clarification in a critical situation between the United States and Mexico and prevent war. As a result he became a sort of prophetic leader for Mexican workers with a powerful influence in other related fields. In cooperation with them and the organized workers of Puerto Rico the American Federation of Labor took leadership in developing a Western Hemisphere organization of trade unions of workers. Their purpose was to extend the constructive power of trade unionism among the workers of the Western Hemisphere to enable them to use their economic power for justice and equal opportunity:

> With the political issues and political factions of Mexico the American labor movement has no vital concern, but it has a deep abiding interest in the growth and progress of the cause of labor in Mexico, and it desires to do all that can be done in a spirit of fraternity and cooperation. The American labor movement recognizes that in the organization of the Mexican workers there lies an element of great hope, for there is a force that has power to shape a great future for a people capable of conceiving great ideas and an understanding of the possibilities which human life can attain when given opportunities and freedom.*

He later amplified:

> From the very beginning of our efforts to promote this Pan-American Federation of Labor one fundamental principle must be thoroughly understood. We, in the United States, concede to Mexico and the people of Mexico the right to work out their own problems according to their own ideals and in accord with their needs and the conditions that exist. We must insist upon the same right for the United States. The American trade union movement must have the sole right to determine the affairs of the American trade union movement. Just as it will be party to no movement to enforce American thought and American institutions upon other peoples, so it can not permit the theories of any other American country to dominate, minimize or change the principles of the American labor movement.*

* American Federationist, July 1916.
* American Federationist, August 1916.

S. G. hoped to be able to show Latin-American workers how to participate in freedom on equal footing with all other citizens—free from dictation from others and free from any delusion of a mission to dictate to others. He hoped to make the Pan American Federation of Labor a supplement to the Pan American Union and to establish the practice of representation for workers in the Union so that they might share in social and cultural progress. He regarded the achievement as the pinnacle of his trade union work thus rounding out the functions of trade unions at all social levels. However, his development of a constructive, conservative domestic labor movement which made possible services at home and abroad was his great contribution to his time, to his country and to wage earners and employers everywhere.

24. A Leader of Men

Mr. Gompers' wisdom was not from books but from personal contacts and exchange of experience and thought with others, frequent and long discussions which helped to avoid fallacies in thought and formulation of plans. In addition he had rare power of drawing from some reservoir of human experience and wisdom—a power essentially primitive and organic—the essence of some spiritual communion. This I felt often and had the rare experience of seeing once. In his leadership in connection with World War I he was most careful to be restrained enough not to be in advance of political leadership, yet positive and forceful enough to help workers not to be misled. He timed his national conference of union executives by President Wilson's schedule, to follow immediately the declaration of war by Congress and to be supplemented by the first meeting of his Advisory Committee on War Labor Problems. Suddenly President Wilson changed his schedule. S.G.'s letters fixing dates of his meetings had gone out. If he held his meetings as planned he might place Labor in the position of declaring war in advance of the Government. To change his dates meant complications and embarrassment because of a commission coming from England. It happened to be my responsibility to convey information of change to him. My eyes were on my memorandum. There was deep silence so intense I looked up with concern. He had turned and sat looking in the opposite direction and somehow had shrunk into himself. His lips moved as he talked with himself—in a sibilant scarcely audible tone. The inner communication with his conscious and subconscious lasted at least fifteen minutes. When his decision was reached he turned and gradually became normal. It was a privacy to be respected—and was. No order to countermand meetings was issued—they were held and were of outstanding service.

S. G. always kept contact with the producing workers. He traveled widely and wherever he went, he made contacts with local people, going off with one or more for a meal or a drink, talking and discussing local problems and whatever was in their minds. This habit enabled him to spot able trade unionists developing and to keep them in mind for future service as well as to make sure they had an understanding of the basic principles of free trade unionism. His mind seized and stored any key information or developing trend. He never disregarded the advice of his pals but modified or even reversed his own thinking accordingly. He could develop the Federation only with the cooperation and active support of its executives and members. It was never in his mind a one-man achievement.

At the national level were experienced and able executives whom he consulted frequently as needful and who helped in guiding the work of conferences and conventions. Convention committee chairmen usually consulted with him freely during conventions and kept him advised on committee reports so that when advisable he could meet with committees. By such teamwork many were educated in the principles and policies of the Federation so that convention discussion occurred between representatives who understood why policies prevailed.

In addition S. G. presided over a convention with an eye to dramatize important events and decisions so they would be remembered. He himself was an actor of no mean calibre—but not just for purposes of display or to carry a point but for an educational purpose of explaining situations. His use of the dramatic was because his very nature was dramatic as well as to reinforce the intense seriousness of his conviction or purposes. He was so supercharged with magnetism that his presence compelled attention. Unwitting "statesmen" occasionally charged him with demagoguery but not for long. His record refuted that charge.

S. G. believed in voluntarism as the way of life for free people with interrelations growing out of mutuality of interest, sustained and directed by dependability, practicality, confidence and good faith. He used all of himself in his various projects with a prodigality that was exhausting—as he said he was a partisan without reserves when the issue was joined—mind, voice, sense of drama, instinct for timing, ability to know his fellowman and what went on in their minds and souls. His mind was stored with information which he could recall and use as needed. His instinct for timing gave him good publicity and emphasized drama.

He could not teach these things by precept but he helped others to learn by observing him if they had the capacities.

Although he did not set any store by formalities he had a very keen sense of personal dignity and resented invasion of his essential privacy by anyone. When his autobiography was in preparation, as often as possible his secretary had his lunch brought in for him to eat in my office so he could go over documents under consideration. One day when that work was finished he went behind the screen before the wash-basin to shave. The office boy had just brought in tree-ripened oranges sold from the truck that brought them up from Florida. The whole situation was quite informal and un-office like—when in strolled Judge Alton B. Parker. The door was open through to S. G.'s office and the unoccupied office of his secretary. Judge Parker chattered with me about his neighbors—the Thornes of New York State—enjoyed an orange, with watchful eye on the silent figure behind the screen. Then appreciative of the feelings behind the screen, with a twinkle in his eye the Judge sauntered into S. G.'s office and sat down. The secretary who had just come back from lunch formally announced the Judge. The short figure emerged bristling with dignity and entered his office —and all was well. He loved and admired the Judge deeply.

Varying degrees of opposition are useful in maintaining healthy leadership. This was readily available through some well-meaning trade unionists who were inclined to look upon political procedures as a way to by-pass economic strikes and conflicts as means to the same ends—higher wages, shorter hours, better working conditions. Gompers and his group urged "pure and simple" trade unionism—organization of workers of the same trades or industries directed by these workers to promote their own interests and welfare. The operation of their voluntary organizations of, by and for the workers taught their members that they must be responsible in order to maintain and use this basic business agency to gain benefits for members. Experience further taught them lasting economic progress must be mutual and that cooperation of all concerned to that end would secure ample for all. Socialist workers argued they must capture political power and enact legislation to gain their union objectives and that a law would benefit all workers whereas a union contract might limit benefits to union members. The debates that followed served to clarify thinking and formulate union policy and traditions. The debates of elder trade unionists became the text books of new members in which they learned the practice of initiative and self-reliance, as well as sound trade union principles. Principles provide moorings so that the whole of life can be consistent and in accord with a directing philosophy. Then common problems —the judiciary usurping legislative functions, the Speaker of the House and his despotic power, etc., served as occasions to discuss basic principles of government and to rally trade unionists for closer unity. They could also have started a drift for disunity—S. G. took no chances and rallied his cohorts periodically.

S. G. took his responsibility of leadership as a serious obligation to serve constructively those he represented and taught them the principles which served him as ground rules:

Trade unions are associations of workers, for workers, by workers to deal with workers' problems of life and work.

Working together on projects develops solidarity and effectiveness through organized collective responsibility.

The ultimate defensive weapon of workers in private employment is the strike and of those in government employment is legislation.

The right to strike is a right of free individuals and is inalienable.

A paid up union card is the credential of union membership, to be recognized by all unions.

The problems and procedure of industrial production are economic in character and are best dealt with by economic procedures and agencies—not political.

One jurisdiction—one union—one control.

Trade unions should use primarily the usual business control—contract—for determining relationships with management and fixing standards of employment in privately owned establishments.

Union representatives elected by workers are their agents in negotiation of contracts as well as in all other union undertakings.

Trade unions should not transfer authority or responsibility to an outside agency. Union political action is partisan to labor principles, not to any political party.

Trade unions can reorganize or adapt existing agencies for emergencies. There is no need of new ones which only create additional problems and confuse lines of authority. Divided authority leads to confusion and may subordinate the union to other than union control.

The nature of man as he was created makes certain rights necessary for him to live according to his conscience. Public law and order as developed through government should recognize opportunity for the exercise of these inalienable rights as the guide to all legislative provisions. Private associations are necessary to establish economic order and to enable individuals to exercise these rights in work relationships. Responsibility is the corollary of rights.

This he believed was the essence of America—the line of opportunity for freedom.

This philosophy applied to trade unionism and its problems gave him his basic policy of voluntarism, from which his concept of the structure and operation of unions evolved. In studying an economic proposal or a legislative draft, his first query always was: Will this suggestion interfere with individual freedom? His second, does it square with the trade union card? He recognized that life in civilized society necessitated responsibility for the use of individual rights with awareness of the rights of others. His next question was: Will the proposal stimulate or retard workers' initiative? Or, will it substitute a dependence on agencies outside of unions and not directly responsive to the will and the judgment of workers?

He and his advisers applied the above basic principles to all other fields in which workers had interests and what he learned he shared with other workers during the years in which he travelled the length and breadth of our country talking to individuals and groups and speaking to audiences. He was practically never alone from choice. As he loved life he felt it must be shared with other humans to be really savored and appreciated.

His singleness of purpose and undeviating philosophy gave force and meaning to his life and the thousands whose lives he influenced. Practical application of his ground rules worked out as follows in lines of action:

1. The nature of man makes individual freedom an inalienable right in order that he may live in accord with his conscience—his conception of moral standards:

That which we call freedom, that which we call liberty, are not tangible things. They are not handed to any people on a silver platter. They are principles, they are questions of the spirit, and the people must have a consciousness that they not only have the term liberty and freedom, but they must have the power and the right to exercise these great attributes of life.*

2. From this principle he derived the philosophy of voluntarism which he implanted in the structure of trade unionism to give it choice, direction and duties. Men must choose for themselves. Men must accept responsibility for the consequences of choice.

3. The trade union or organization of wage-earners to control their economic power—power to produce—is the agency by which they make their right to choice effective. This power ultimately rests upon their decision to withhold their labor power—that is to supply or man production machinery.

4. Provisions under which labor power is supplied should be prescribed by contracts between management and union executives. These contracts take on the force of obligations through the consent of the workers and employers.

5. The union, the contract with management and machinery for carrying out rules and provisions constitute the means to industrial order. The wants and the rights of the human beings who carry out work orders develop with the quality and breadth of understanding which character-

* Address, National Security League, Chicago, September 14, 1917.

izes this order. The union has the special function of defining the rights of workers as required by natural law which is unwritten law, and of establishing recognition of these rights. Correlation of attendant obligations evolves out of experience which the union accumulates and interprets.

6. The trade union should top the hierarchy of agencies serving wage-earners so that their economic, political, social and cultural progress may be directed and coordinated by a basic philosophy of life. Effective, practical ability to get results rests finally on economic power which in the case of wage-earners is channelled through economic associations —unions.

By lodging final power and decision with the membership of trade unions which are voluntary organizations all human safeguards against arbitrary action and dictatorship were provided. Even more important safeguards consist in the preservation of spiritual forces and moral standards. Unions like all other human organizations must rely upon the calibre of the leaders and the sturdiness of their own moral fibre for refreshment of the spirit and recharging of ideals. This was a necessity of which Mr. Gompers was ever mindful in written, spoken and personal communications.

Never did he speak lightly of or in belittling terms of trade unionism. It was his field of service—his religion.

One wonders whether Gompers' leadership would have been more effective had he acknowledged specifically forces outside the individual and of a higher order which give authority to moral law and commandments. In human relations the commandment to love one another when accepted as a way of life prescribed by the Supreme Intelligence many call God, leads to a higher level of living for which personal freedom is a preparatory first step. Individual freedom is essential to human progress but unless exercised with love and respect for the rights of others may result in individual egotism and lead to social and individual injustices. Belief in authority that transcends human development which the individual senses and acknowledges develops a reverence in living that makes for wisdom in judgment and action. Had Gompers lived to see the trend of present day progress, liberty and human perfectibility would he not have fully accepted and advocated need for a rule of law outside and above the individual and the state—a system of moral absolutes under the guidance of Divine Authority?

APPRECIATION OF THE SPIRIT OF SERVICE

S. G. fully appreciated that without ideals and sentiment the labor movement would soon become merely a tool necessary for material gains. To provide food for the spirit was the purpose back of systematic inclusion in all his annual reports of sections of appreciative reminders of the services of unpaid organizers, the labor press and fitting celebration of special labor days.

In appreciation of the work of organizers he wrote in an annual report:

The most real things in life are not the tangible things we can see and touch, but they are the influences that make the spirit reverent and sweet and true, the glimpses we catch of the meaning of life, the conceptions that have left the trivial and have lost themselves in the immortal and the impersonal—the great motive powers that are felt throughout the ages. The passions, the ambitions, the yearnings of men for something better and higher are the most real things in the life of the people—nay, they are the throbbing, pulsating heart of life itself. Though so vital, so powerful, they are so fine and subtle that we are often unconscious of their presence; yet in the silent and lone places of life, in the times when we test our dreams and visions whether they be in tune with the ultimate and the infinite these real things ring out like some rare strain of sweet music that thrills, and soothes, and comforts. Were it not for the courage and the inspiration born of deeper insight and fuller understanding of the meaning and the process of life and progress, the pain and disappointment would be too overpowering. But these glimpses when eternity affirms the conception of the present are the greatest reward granted honest, true work. If those whose faithful, often unnoted, services have given form and reality to that most real thing in the lives of those who bear the dead weight and burden of America's progress could but sense and realize the full nobility and grandeur of the structure they have reared, infinite peace and satisfaction would be their compensation.

In the hearts and the lives of the working people of America has been builded a Temple of Labor—a structure that has been reared in pain and privation, though it towers upward into the hope-filled sunny skies. Each stone of the great structure was laid by some humble workingman—some were laid in the darkness, some in the dewy morn, some were laid in weariness and pain, some at the cost of rest and leisure, some in the exaltation which comes from unselfish efforts to help the less fortunate. Many who laid the stones may be unknown or forgotten, but each stone is essential to the Temple of Labor—the temple where humanity may enter in and find protection and aid. Those who are weary and heavy laden may enter this Temple of Labor and find comfort and aid in carrying their burdens. In the temple it is the law that men shall possess their own souls in the fulness of freedom and may stretch up to full stature of individual liberty, free from compulsion or oppression.

Such is the Temple of Labor—a temple not made with hands, but by the hearts and lives of human beings. This is the dwelling place of the Spirit of Labor, the creative force, the genius of the brain and the brawn of men, the power that generates freedom and individuality. Those who laid the foundations of this temple, who hewed and fashioned the stones, and carried the blocks and the mortar, are the faithful band of volunteer workers who go among the toilers, tell the story of organization, and show their fellow-workers how the better things of life can be gained. Year after year faithful unpaid organizers have used their leisure time that they might organize the unorganized or add strength and give inspiration to those who might otherwise have lost courage. The labor movement among the American workers is the result of self-sacrifice and consecration of minds and hearts to the work of bettering humanity. Though the individual work may seem inconsequential and scarcely worth while, yet the whole looms big with hope and power—the whole is impossible without each individual endeavor, however unimportant it may seem when isolated. It is their faithful, often wholly unrewarded, endeavors that have given reality to the labor movement—the real Temple of Labor where men may do honor and reverence to the good and the ideal that are in mankind, to the infinite possibilities enveloped in every human life, and where many are enabled to realize the desires of the heart and mind. The appreciation and gratitude of organized labor for the work of those who builded and are building the temple can not be too generous.*

Labor Day and Labor Sunday he interpreted thus:

For every cause there must be something that lifts it out of an atmosphere of common experience and acceptance as a matter of course. The labor movement is an outgrowth of every-day experience; it is intensely practical and seeks certain material ends, but it is guided by ideals that are exalted and illuminated with a realization of the value of life and the possibilities for human development. By

* 1913 Convention Proceedings, Report of the Executive Council, p. 90.

our recognition of these ideals and by keeping them prominently before the workers and the public we set our own valuation upon Labor Day as an index to the value of the movement. Organized labor can not afford, for any reason, to permit the day to lose its real meaning. Whatever may be the cost in money, time and energy is repaid by the inspiration gained from the assembling in mass meetings, demonstrations, and for parades, and the sense of community of interests and fraternity that comes from the personal contact of those working for the same cause.*

He instituted the practice of the convention's listing the names of trade unionists who had died in the interim since the previous convention and then standing in silence for a minute—a wordless testament of appreciation.

S. G. firmly believed that something akin to appreciative meditation was necessary to the health and sustained progress of a movement. He wrote thus of the dignity of labor:

Out in the world of labor and life the workers have put a real meaning into the phrase "the Dignity of Labor" . . . They . . . have expended the best in life and spirit on the work of the world. It has given the dignity of labor a deeper and more permanent expression in the ideals of humanity, justice and freedom, that the workers have been made a part of the guiding and directing forces of our nation. . . . They supply the creative power that is a necessary part of the processes of material production. The work of their hands and brain is everywhere—buildings of industry and railroads that unite the distant parts of our country, the material agencies of transportation and communication, articles of daily food, use and wear, and in all of that which pertains to the material agencies of life and work. They have contributed something more than mechanical producing power, it is the mind and the insight controlling the muscles of the workers that give them value as producers and as members of society. . .*

In his last days in a last talk with a trusted "pal"— James Duncan, Scotch President of the Granite Cutters' International— he charged him with this message to America's wage earners:

Say to them that as I kept the faith I expect they will keep the faith. They must carry on. Say to them that a union man carrying

* 1913 Convention Proceedings, report Executive Council, pp. 96–97.
* American Federationist, February 1916.

a card is not a good citizen unless he upholds the institutions of our great country, and a poor citizen of our country if he upholds the institutions of our country and forgets the obligations of his trade association.*

Those who observed the last convention over which he presided were deeply impressed with the reverence and the love which the delegates expressed in their realization it was the Chief's last council with them. He thanked them for their "graciousness"—and the term was deeply appropriate.

To the last he was concerned with the principles of human freedom. In the great park just out of Mexico City where he went for rest in the sunshine, the boatmen and gardeners hovered round him and instinctively knelt at his feet—blessing him for their freedom. He had made them free and had given them the bread of life.

He was rushed from Mexico to San Antonio to fulfill his wish to die in the United States. His last journey—from San Antonio to Washington, D.C.—was a testament of deep national respect and love—the maintenance-of-way workers as they watched his passing, groups of people in towns where the train stopped came with expressions of love and loss, and where the train went through without stop stood in wordless appreciation of the leader whose life had been service through love of life and fellowship.

In memoriam of him the Executive Council said:

We realize that his leadership was based upon an understanding of permanent values and that his death has revealed the spiritual forces which directed his work and which he fostered and developed in the labor movement. In the great cause of human emancipation the work of Samuel Gompers supplemented that of Abraham Lincoln and established new goals and new ideals of democracy in our common life. The spirit of Samuel Gompers is permanently a part of the world's constructive ideals and forces for human welfare.*

* American Federationist, January 1925.
* American Federationist, January 1925.

Bibliography

Seventy Years of Life and Labor, by Samuel Gompers.
An autobiography completed just before his death.
E. P. Dutton & Co., 1925.

Convention Proceedings of the American Federation of Labor, (Annual) 1881 - 1924.

American Federationist, 1894 - 1925. Official magazine, American Federation of Labor. Samuel Gompers, Editor, 1894, 1896 - 1924.

A. F. of L. Headquarters
Some incoming correspondence, 1881 - 1897.
Complete file copy books for out-going letters, 1897 - 1924.
Official files indexed by years and subjects.
Gompers special files.
File of speeches collected by Miss Guard, his secretary.
Minutes of Executive Council Meetings.
Gompers Engagement Books.

The Origins of International Labor Organization, James T. Shotwell.

Hidden Threads of History—Louis B. Wehle. Macmillan.

Hearing (H. J. 159, April 11, 1915) Committee on Labor, U.S. House of Representatives, and

Selected Hearings on Injunction and Anti-Trust Bills.

Astor Library, New York City.
(Mr. Gompers' will directed his secretary and the author to dispose of his personal papers. These were deposited in the Astor Library in the city which had been his home and voting residence.)
Duplicate file of speeches, special articles and press releases.
Scrap books kept by Samuel Gompers or Miss Guard.
Collection of clippings.
Occasional personal memorandum.

175